SAMUEL TAYLOR COLERIDGE

Andrew Keanie

GREENWICH EXCHANGE
LONDON

Greenwich Exchange, London

First published in Great Britain in 2002

Printed and bound by Q3 Digital/Litho, Loughborough
Tel: 01509 213456
Typesetting and layout by Albion Associates, London
Tel: 020 8852 4646
Cover design by December Publications, Belfast
Tel: 028 90352059

Cover photograph: © Hulton Images

Greenwich Exchange Website: www.greenex.co.uk

ISBN 1-871551-64-1

My babe so beautiful! it thrills my heart
With tender gladness, thus to look at thee,
And think that thou shalt learn far other lore,
And in far other scenes!
Coleridge 'Frost At Midnight'

For Emma, with love.

Contents

Chronology

1772   Coleridge born, 21st October, Ottery St Mary, Devonshire.

1781   Coleridge's father, Revd John Coleridge, dies.

1782   Coleridge enrolls at Christ's Hospital, London.

1791   Jesus College, Cambridge.

1792   Writes prizewinning Greek Sapphic 'Ode on the Slave-Trade'.

1793   First poem published in *Morning Chronicle*. Leaves Cambridge. Joins Light Dragoons under pseudonym.

1794   Discharged. Goes back to Cambridge. Meets Thomas Poole. Meets Robert Southey. Leaves Cambridge with no degree.

1795   Lectures in Bristol. Beginning of sustained fantasy of 'Pantisocracy' with Southey. Marries Southey's sister-in-law-to-be, Sarah Fricker.

1796   *Watchman* – democratic periodical lasts for ten issues. Coleridge's son, Hartley, born.

1797   Meets Dorothy and William Wordsworth. Begins *Rime of the Ancient Mariner*. Completes first (best) part of 'Christabel'. Writes 'Kubla Khan'. (Initially, use of opium plays a part in yielding wonderful poetic results.)

1798   Coleridge's second son, Berkeley, born. Completes *Rime*. Joint collection of poems (with Wordsworth) published anonymously. Dorothy, William and Coleridge go to Germany.

1799   Meets Humphry Davy in Bristol. Coleridge and Davy experiment with nitrous oxide. Meets Wordsworth's future sister-in-law – the woman with whom Coleridge would be utterly besotted for many unhappy years – 'Asra' (Sara Hutchinson).

1800	Moves to Greta Hall, Keswick. Derwent Coleridge born. Coleridge completes second part of 'Christabel'. Sees second edition of *Lyrical Ballads* through press.
1802	Sara Coleridge born. Coleridge publishes 'Dejection: An Ode'.
1803	Hopelessly addicted to opium.
1804-6	In Malta.
1807	Meets De Quincey. Hears Wordsworth recite *Prelude*.
1809	*The Friend* – periodical lasts for 27 issues. This is the project on which Coleridge's 'Asra' acts as his amanuensis for the last time.
1810	Huge quarrel with Wordsworth.
1811	Lectures on Shakespeare.
1813	Coleridge's *Remorse* runs for 20 nights in London. (His successes as a lecturer and a playwright have given him celebrity status in the capital.)
1814	Stays with the Morgans at Ashley. Begins *Biographia Literaria*.
1816	Taken in by physician, James Gillman. Will stay with Gillman, at Highgate, for the rest of his life. 'Kubla Khan' and 'Christabel' published.
1817	*Biographia Literaria* published.
1825	*Aids to Reflection* published.
1834	Having spent much of his adulthood filling astonishing private notebooks, Coleridge dies at Highgate (25th July).

1895	A selection from Coleridge's notebook entries, *Anima Poetae* (edited by E.H. Coleridge), published.
1928	A young scholar (Kathleen Coburn) of Victoria College, University of Toronto, inspired by John Livingston Lowes's *Road to Xanadu*, develops a passion for the writings of STC.
1961	Coleridge re-buried in Highgate Parish Church.

1　His Father's Son

I　Habituated to the Vast

> I read every book that came in my way without distinction –
> and my father was very fond of me, & used to take me on his
> knee, and hold long conversations with me. I remember, that
> at eight years old I walked with him one evening from a
> farmer's house, a mole from Ottery – & he told me the names
> of the stars – and how Jupiter was a thousand times larger
> than our world – and that the other twinkling stars were Suns
> that had worlds rolling around them – & when I came home,
> he shewed me how they rolled round –. I heard him with a
> profound delight & admiration; but without the least mixture
> of wonder or incredulity. For from my early reading of Faery
> Tales, & Genii etc. etc. – my mind had been *habituated to the
> Vast* ...

Attempting to vindicate his fecklessness in practical affairs and as
evidence of his other-worldliness, Coleridge would fondly recall his
youthful voracious book-reading, and his father's benevolent
immersion of his son – the eight-year-old Sam – in science, fantasy
and philosophy. Coleridge's intellectual life continued in the fashion
started by his father. The open-minded Greek atomists' belief in the
multiplicity of things, and the rise of modern science in Renaissance
Europe with its refutation of Aristotle's view that the earth lay at the
centre of a spherical cosmos, would be among the many 'caverns
measureless to man' explored by Coleridge.

"I compose very little – and I absolutely hate composition. Such
is my dislike, that even a sense of Duty is sometimes too weak to
overpower it." Coleridge was unable to play the writer – to himself,
in his study – to have left behind the body of work that he should. "I
am a Starling self-incaged, & always in the Moult, & my whole
Note is, Tomorrow, & tomorrow, & tomorrow." He was to often
incapable of suspending his own disbelief to settle down, write and
finish a work of literature.

The brilliant, often shambolic, radical lectures he delivered in
Bristol in the early 1790s embodied republicanism at it most inspired

and least efficient; the poems he contributed to his and William Wordsworth's epoch-changing collection, *Lyrical Ballads* (1798), were, in his own (later) words, "an interpolation of heterogeneous matter"; the notebooks he kept would have to be sifted tirelessly into readability by the Canadian scholar, Kathleen Coburn, during the mid to late twentieth century. The following is an excerpt from Coburn's report to her publisher, in 1951, which conveys something of the disordered state of the notebooks as she had first found them:

> The Notebooks run to rather more than a million words and the entries are in chaos. They need to be put in chronological order. There was no sort of system, chronological or topical; and the first and most difficult and most time-consuming task, after the transcription, is the dating and ordering of the entries. Some of the writing is difficult – faded pencil, rain and sea water stains, careless writing, one entry superimposed on another, entries in cypher, these are some of the difficulties. Other problems require the help of persons with special knowledge of recondite Greek, German, and Italian, and the history of science and theology. The resources of the largest libraries will be required.

Much of Coleridge's genius was simply not presentable. It has had to be unearthed from itself by the labours of convinced Coleridgeans.

His (indeed England's) greatest treatise on Romanticism – *Biographia Literaria* (1817) – is a sustained effusion of cultured, extravagant digressions in and around the subjects of Coleridge himself and what Coleridge had read ('everything') and thought. In it, he acknowledges his own good fortune to have been endowed with imagination and intellect of almost Shakespearean dimensions. But, at the same time, he also addresses his misfortune to have possessed the kind of – sadly – intermittent focus responsible for carrying his muse too erratically between conception and delivery.

Years after Coleridge had written his most powerful poems – such as 'Kubla Khan', the first part of 'Christabel', and *The Rime of the Ancient Mariner* – the critic, William Hazlitt, asserted that, "If Mr Coleridge had not been the most impressive talker of his age, he would probably have been the finest writer ..." Then again, Hazlitt's innate nastiness – all the more necessary because Coleridge had always been very kind to him as a younger man – has long been one of the firmly established facts of Romantic research. (Stephen Gill and A.S. Byatt have been among recent writers on the Wordsworth/ Coleridge circle to mention it.) The poet himself implied that, painful though it was to be punished publicly by others for not having converted enough of his creative energy into literature of lasting significance, it was as nothing compared to how hard he would be on himself: "By what I *have* effected, am I to be judged by my fellow men, what I *could* have done, is a question for my own conscience." Of course, this also means mind your own business.

The radically minded, widely read tanner, Tom Poole, formed the following first impression of the young Coleridge:

> He speaks with much elegance and energy, and with un-common facility, but he, as it generally happens to men of his class, feels the justice of Providence in the want of those inferior abilities which are necessary to the rational discharge of the common duties of life.

Later on, having become familiar, through friendship, with some of the psychological nuances of the mercurial Coleridge, a more fatherly Poole would write to advise the great poet. Poole (writing from England) hoped that Coleridge (sojourning in Germany) was working hard at garnering the fruits of German metaphysics, not frittering his talents away attended by a clique of admiring under-graduates at Göttingen:

> Make a strict arrangement of your time and chain yourself down to it ... It would counteract a *disease* of your mind – which is an active subtlety of imagination ... This many of your friends falsely call irresolution. No one has more resolution than you.

This was in 1798: an attempt at finger-wagging conjoined with praise – the fond hope being that Coleridge would heed him. If only that – by turns industrious and dissolute – young Coleridge would avail of this unique opportunity during his few months in Germany! Poole was one of the many whose letters to, and about, Coleridge, bespeak something of the torture endured by parents watching their beloved prodigal son – for whom they have high hopes – make a mess of things. There is the emphatically asserted game-plan; the nervous, pleading rigidity; the love:

> You are now, dear Col, fixed in Germany, and what you have to do is to attend *wholly* to those things that are better attained in Germany than elsewhere... I should spend no time to send anything to Stuart ... *Begin* no poetry – no original composition – unless translation from German may be so called ... Beware of being too much with Chester ... Live with Germans. Read in German. Think in German.

Coleridge would play one part for the benefit of, say, his patrons, Josiah and Tom Wedgwood; another for, say, his gifted, eccentric admirer, the essayist Charles Lamb; and another for, say, the political philosopher, William Godwin. In a lifelong effort to get them to do (usually practical) things for him that he could not (or would not) do for himself, Coleridge elicited love from different people with his protean eloquence.

The biographer, Richard Holmes, shrewdly suggests that, in order to fund the immediate enterprise of being 'all things to all men', the young Coleridge compelled Providence to grant him a loan from his life's remaining quantum of nervous energy. Coleridge's loss – that is, his failure to execute as many great works as he should have – was the interest he had to pay. Pursuing the metaphor, the interest he paid was the disordered state of his accounts (unfinished poems such as 'Christabel' and grand metaphysical prose projects never begun), and permanent and increasing deficits that he would make good.

A little later in his career, Coleridge would take stock of the unsightly half-accomplishments littering his conscience. Comparing his achievement with that of the deeply meditative piety of the metaphysical poet, George Herbert, and finding the former wanting, Coleridge drifted somewhat guiltily:

> ... it needs only that I should be left to myself to sink into the chaos and lawless productivity of my own still perishing yet imperishable nature.

Yet, his negative, emotional energy was being harnessed in a fresh way. The sense of failure was often Coleridge's trade wind before

4

which his words advantageously ran ('perishing … imperishable'): this exemplified Romanticism.

It was not just the immensity of the cosmos that occupied his thoughts – he concerned himself, just as habitually, with the minutiae that ultimately make up the Whole. Look at his first notebook entry:

> Think any number you like – double – add 12 to it – halve it
> – take away the original number – and there remains six –

Try this: it is the strangeness, that this really is an arithmetical truth, that seized Coleridge's imagination. Or rather, its strangeness seized his imagination for a short, intense time, before his imagination shot off in the direction of quite other beacon-fires. Take this observation – a notebook entry from December 1801:

> Feel a pimple, and measure it – *feeling* – & then look at it –
> how very small it is compared with what you expected it to
> be. So measure one of your teeth at the edge with your finger,
> what a breadth – Explain this diversity of *feeling* & sight.

His instinctive appetite for knowledge meant a childhood and young adulthood crammed with reading. His mind was nevertheless capacious enough to assimilate it and so make it contribute to the organic unity of his insight – which is actually his greatest achievement. He even became, almost in passing, by his mid/late twenties, a truly scientific thinker of some standing. His learning was staggering to others, but of insufficient account to himself – he was after all "habituated *to the Vast*" – he was never 'comfortable' – there was always more to learn.

It is testimony to Coleridge's uniqueness that Richard Dawkins (the zoologist/militant atheist who usually relishes the job of withering the persistent arguments of creationists) treats the erstwhile Unitarian preacher without his customary, rancorously persuasive ridicule. "We must," says the debunker of cosmic sentimentality with a suspiciously brisk air of calmness, "set [Coleridge] on one side as a unique anomaly, and move on." [*Unweaving the Rainbow* (1998).] It could be argued that Dawkins, the aggressive populariser of 'Darwinian' evolution, has been made aware by Coleridge, of the possibility that a human being is not, like all other individual organisms, *just* a survival mechanism for genes. Later in his book, Dawkins admires a striking passage from one of Coleridge's notebooks accurately communicating the "illusion of the rainbow itself [that] remains rock steady, although the drops that deliver it are scurrying about in the wind." If Coleridge's spell is powerful enough to echo through the centuries, via his apparently confused notebook ramblings, and make a *Dawkins* pause for thought, it is easy to understand the hypnotic effect that the poet is reported to have had upon his pre-Darwin contemporaries.

William Godwin, 16 years Coleridge's senior, converted from atheism as a direct result of his frequent conversations with Coleridge. The young William Hazlitt wrote that, "There is a *chaunt* in the recitation both of Coleridge and Wordsworth, which acts as a spell upon the hearer, and disarms judgement ..." Hazlitt also wrote that Coleridge's genius "had angelic wings and fed on manna. He talked on for ever; and you wished him to talk on for ever ..." In 1815, the literary lawyer, Sir Thomas Noon Talfourd, wrote that, "In spell poetry [Coleridge] is far more potent than any writer of the present age, – his enchantments are more marvellous and deeper woven, – his fictions wilder, – and his mysteries more heart-touching and appalling." Coleridge was a charming performance poet and conversationalist. Some of that charm, after a couple of centuries, has reached us intact.

But he was also 'wonderful'. Dorothy Wordsworth called him "a wonderful man", and William called him this on hearing of his death. The Wordsworths did not use words like this lightly. Dorothy's account of her first meeting with Coleridge captures something of his presence:

> His conversation teems with soul, mind, and spirit ... At first I thought him very plain, that is, for about three minutes: he ... has a wide mouth, thick lips, and not very good teeth, longish loose-growing half-curling rough black hair. But if you hear him speak for five minutes you think no more of them. His eye is large and full, not dark but grey; such an eye as would receive from a heavy soul the dullest expression; but it speaks every emotion of his animated mind; it has more of the 'poet's eye in a fine frenzy rolling' than I ever witnessed. He has fine dark eyebrows, and an overhanging forehead.

6

William Hazlitt's account of his own, first-hand experience of a fully inspired Coleridge, is one of the most powerful pen-portraits of genius. Hazlitt sets the desolate, wintry scene of his own, personal circumstances, and then, with the benefit of hindsight, blows a rousing verbal fanfare to herald the arrival of Coleridge into the consciousness of a gifted young man:

> It was in January, 1798, that I rose one morning before day-light, to walk ten miles in the mud, and went to hear this celebrated person preach. Never, the longest day I have to live, shall I have such another walk as this cold, raw, comfortless one, in the winter of the year 1798 ... When I got there, the organ was playing the 100th psalm, and, when it was done, Mr. Coleridge rose and gave out his text, 'And he went up into the mountains to pray, HIMSELF ALONE.' As he gave out his text, his voice 'rose like a steam of rich distilled perfumes', and when he came to the two last words, which he pronounced loud, deep, and distinct, it seemed to me, who was then young, as if the sounds had echoed from the bottom of the human heart, and as if that prayer might have floated in solemn silence through the universe. The idea of St John came into mind, 'of one crying in the wilderness, who had his loins girt about, and whose food was locusts and wild honey'. The preacher then launched into his subject, like an eagle dallying with the wind. The sermon was upon peace and war; upon church and state – not their alliance, but their separation – on the spirit of the world and the spirit of Christianity, not as the same, but as opposed to one another. He talked of those who had 'inscribed the cross of Christ on banners dripping with human gore'. He made a poetical and pastoral excursion, – and to shew the fatal effects of war, drew a striking contrast between the simple shepherd boy, driving his team afield, or sitting under the hawthorn, piping to his flock, 'as though he should never be old', and the same poor country-lad, crimped, kidnapped, brought into town, made drunk at an alehouse, turned into a wretched drummer-boy, with his hair sticking on end with powder and pomatum, a long cue at his back, and tricked out in the loathsome finery of the profession of blood.
> 'Such were the notes our once-lov'd poet sung'.

Hazlitt's reaction is telling:

And for myself, I could not have been more delighted if I had heard the music of the spheres. Poetry and Philosophy had met together. Truth and Genius had embraced, under the eye and with the sanction of Religion. This was even beyond my hopes. I returned home well satisfied. The sun that was still labouring pale and wan through the sky, obscured by thick mists, seemed an emblem of the *good cause*; and the cold dank drops of dew that hung half melted on the beard of the thistle, had something genial and refreshing in them; for there was a spirit of hope and youth in all nature, that turned every thing into good.

Hazlitt had begun, above, by evoking his own *pre-Coleridge* loneliness in order then to throw into relief, faithfully, the colourful contagiousness of Coleridgean inspiration. (Why did Coleridge preach? To be like, or to reach out to, his dead father who had habituated his mind "*to the Vast*"?) Coleridge had the power to inspire Hazlitt and send him back to the world of ordinary, everyday things with new eyes.

The following, from an 1811-12 notebook entry of Coleridge, possesses the same assertion of wonder and excitement as the late twentieth century's handful of gifted 'Popular Science' writers such as Carl Sagan, Paul Davies, Stephen Jay Gould, or even Isaac Asimov could convey:

What a swarm of thoughts and feelings, endlessly minute fragments, and, as it were, representations of all preceding and embryos of all future thought, lie compact in any one moment! So, in a single drop of water, the microscope discovers what motions, what tumult, what wars, what pursuits, what stratagems, what a circle-dance of death and life, death-hunting life, and life renewed and invigorated by death! The whole world seems here in a many-meaning cypher. What if our existence was but that moment? What an unintelligible, affrightful riddle, what a chaos of limbs and trunk, tailless, headless, nothing begun and nothing ended, would it not be? And yet scarcely more than that other moment of fifty or sixty years, were that our all? Each part throughout infinite diminution adapted to some other, and yet the whole a means to nothing – ends everywhere, and yet an end nowhere.

Conspicuously erudite on all subjects, Coleridge had the ability to assimilate and synthesise, with a journalistic sparkle for which most writers would kill. Sara, Coleridge's daughter, had this to say, not long after Coleridge's death:

> It does not seem as if the writer was especially conversant with this or that, as [Charles] Babbage [the inventor of the calculating machine that anticipated the modern computer] with mechanics, and [John Stuart] Mill with political economy; but as if there was a subtle imaginative spirit to search and illustrate all subjects that interest humanity.

Coleridge was, like his father, a Renaissance man, conversant equally with the voices of literary antiquity as well as those of contemporary science. His father had been an adorable, quixotic character: Coleridge was the same – and he cultivated it to get people to love him. This would explain why Coleridge was so scruffily presented, at his Bristol lectures, as to excite comment in the printed reviews. The *Observer* lamented his dirty stockings, tangled hair, and generally 'slovenly' presence, depreciatingly offset as he was by the spick-and-span Southey, who displayed a crisp professionalism as a lecturer. But there was coherence between presentation and content. The *Observer* also expressed distaste at Coleridge's dreamy digressions – those absent-minded, intellectual leaps over the abyss of irrelevance, that often irritate down-to-earth (paying) members of an audience. However, cultivation of eccentricity aside, Richard Holmes appreciates the catholic Coleridge's informed enthusiasm: "he seemed to learn as much from landscapes as from literature; as much from children's games as from philosophic treatises; as much from bird-flight as from theology."

In her book, *In Pursuit of Coleridge* (1977), Kathleen Coburn recalls her arduous navigation of the ocean of Coleridge's work, as she, and her team, transcribed the notebooks:

> Some entries were difficult because of the impossibility of anticipating Coleridge's vocabulary ... But one striking fact about the entries having to do with writers and thinkers was that, whatever his attitude, the relationship to them was intimate, real, a shared inheritance, a felt intellectual drive; he sought a common climate even with opponents.

In *Confessions of an English Opium-Eater* (1821), Thomas De Quincey's estimation of Coleridge's talent has more of the (valuable) alertness to the defects of a contemporary competitor:

> But the truth is, that inaccuracy as to facts and citations from books was in Coleridge a mere necessity of nature. Not three days ago, in reading a short comment of the late Arch-deacon Hare (*Guesses at Truth*) upon a bold speculation of Coleridge's (utterly baseless) with respect to the machinery of Etonian Latin verses, I found my old feelings upon the subject refreshed by an instance that is irresistibly comic, since everything that Coleridge had relied upon as a citation from a book in support of his own hypothesis, turns out to be a pure fabrication of his own dreams; though, doubtless (which indeed it is that constitutes the characteristic interest of the case), without a suspicion on his part of his own furious romancing.

However right he may have been for quizzically discussing Coleridge's "venial infirmity", it is possible that, as Coleridge's contemporary, De Quincey was standing too close to him to be able to take the full measure of his genius.

Prolonged exposure to the works of Coleridge may romanticise the perceptions of even the most hardened reductionist into a state of *aching for wholeness*. One may be an 'expert' on the subject of quantum physics; another may be a particularly knowledgeable chemist ... but how do all these bits and pieces add up? What about that *whole* that is the universe?

> I have known some who have been *rationally* educated, as it is styled. They were marked by a microscopic acuteness; but when they looked at great things, all became a blank & they saw nothing ... and uniformly put the negation of a power for the possession of a power – & called the want of imagination, Judgment, & the never being moved to Rapture Philosophy!

The sense of this passage should not be lost. There is a sharp line of demarcation between the handful of geniuses and the millions of ordinary people concerned with solving life's riddles. The 25 year old poet's prose has crackled into far-reaching significance because he has just been jolted with the realisation that he is definitely a genius. Regarding the birth of a work of genius, as long as the artist is in a susceptible mood (for Wordsworth it was a "wise passiveness"; for Keats it would be "Negative Capability"), almost any object that comes within range of his perceptions will begin to speak. The sight of the object will generate some lively, penetrating and original thought. So it is that a trivial event may become the seed of a great and glorious work. There is a notebook entry (written in 1810) in which Coleridge formulates this thought, which could easily have become post-Kantian rigmarole in lesser hands:

> Man of genius places things in *a new light* – this trivial phrase better expresses the appropriate efforts of Genius than Pope's celebrated Distich – What oft was thought but ne'er so well exprest. It had been *thought* DISTINCTLY, but only possessed, as it were, unpacked & unsorted – the poet not only *displays* what tho often seen in its unfolded mass had never been opened out, but he likewise adds something, namely, Lights & Relations. – who has not seen a Rose, or a sprig of Jasmine, of Myrtle, etc. etc.? – But behold these same flowers in a posy or flowerpot, painted by a man of genius – or assorted by the hand of a woman of fine Taste & instinctive sense of Beauty?

It would certainly not be any actual experience that would sow within Coleridge the seed of, say, *The Rime of the Ancient Mariner*: he had not travelled on any sea voyage by the time *The Rime* was written. The expansion of poetic genius in pursuit of Truth may have its starting point *anywhere*, however humdrum, before being borne on the rhapsodic currents of inexplicable momentum. In one of his many notebook aphorisms, Coleridge would (in December 1797) indicate the limitations of a certain kind of book-learning: "Snails of intellect, who see only with their Feelers ..."

II   Thoroughgoing Radical

In 1793, he began to cultivate his notoriety, in Bristol, by giving a series of lectures whose principles were cordially republican. And republican idealism was now paying heavily, in England, for the atrocities in France. However, Coleridge was a thick-skinned, witty performer. The disruptive booing and hissing of knee-jerk conservatives once sprang the following Coleridgean trap: "I am not at all surprised, when the red hot prejudices of aristocrats are suddenly plunged into the cool waters of reason, that they should go off with a hiss!" This is a satisfyingly waggish retort. (He would later find this notoriety extremely difficult to shake off.) But it is made much more interesting in the light of Coleridge's obsession with science. The young Coleridge's precocious use of scientific analogies loosely aligned him with the feisty malcontents who had recently pamphleteered England into a fizz of political paranoia. From a local perspective, Bristol's conservative contingent did not want this "damn'd Jacobin ... jawing away" in his subversively eloquent Devon accent. In the wider political context, scientific research boosted the stockpile of metaphors to be used by left-wing writers (and, it would soon come to be the consensus that poets worth their salt were, in the tradition of Milton, politically antagonistic thinkers).

Another source of political metaphors for the radical young lecturer lies in maritime imagery. Anyone even vaguely familiar with the slightly older Coleridge's *Rime of the Ancient Mariner* (1798) will quickly recognise the prospect:

> When the Wind is fair and the planks of the vessel sound, we may safely trust everything to the management of professional Mariners; but in a Tempest and on board a crazy Bark, all must contribute their Quota of Exertion. The Stripling is not exempted from it by his Youth, not the Passenger by his Inexperience. Even so in the present agitations of the Public mind, everyone ought to consider his intellectual faculties as in a *state of requisition*.

Coleridge opened his first lecture with the above. With verve and audacity, he honed his penmanship (and his charismatically unkempt, left-wing-intellectual appearance) on the polemically inflamed symptoms of conservative anxiety.

In a letter, he describes his friend, Robert Southey, in political terms, but more with the relish of writing talent conscious of its own increasing strength and fitness: "He is truly a man of *perpendicular Virtue – a down-right upright republican!*" Coleridge's drollery and his enjoyment in writing it unmistakably permeates this faintly absurd phrase.

III   The Emerging Writer

For all his flaunted republicanism, the young Coleridge was really more interested in the play of words and phrases with which he aspired to flourish his thoughts into far-reaching significance. The following notebook entry (1803) presents, in peculiarly Coleridgean bullet-point form, the progression of the genius in the direction of immortality:

> The heat of fermentation from the warmth of Life/the bustling Dotage of Composition & the calm long-subsequent admiration/

The second point is telling. Coleridge is writing about himself in the process of composition. The very high level of mental activity, as he composes, is hidden by what an external observer would perceive as wholly unwarranted self-absorption, and cross-grained incompetence. (Remember Tom Poole's first perception, amounting to the view of Coleridge as a Pegasus in terms of intellect, but an ass in terms of "the rational discharge of the common duties of life.") There is no guarantee that anyone who shares his or her life with a writer will be able to tolerate the symptoms of serious thought. There is, for example, the jealously guarded space for working, and the smells of tobacco, coffee/tea, and old books that it hermetically seals. There is the sight of apparently meaningless scribbles in grubby looking (yet ferociously protected) notebooks. And, in general, there is the glamour-free *uncoolness* of the writer's lot. The writer may have refined an elaborate, if eccentric, system of cross-referencing that accommodates his – and *only* his – peculiar quirkiness of thought. But outwardly, he has not combed his hair, nor wiped this morning's egg off his shirtfront; nor has he remembered to put the same coloured sock on each foot; and, of course, there are the maturing debts, and children ... Now, if the writer's wife suspects that he is actually 'acting-up' this aspect of his personality, the potential for the household stock-in-trade – the domestic row – is not likely to diminish. Mrs Sarah Coleridge must be due our sympathy. By 1799, she must have been baffled and annoyed by what would have appeared to her to be the unpardonable indolence of her husband. Imagine Sarah finding, and reading, this letter, cheerfully penned by a husband whose family would better have needed an energetic, provider father-figure:

> ... it [opium] leaves my sensitive Frame *so* sensitive! My enjoyments are so deep, of the fire, of the Candle, of the thought I am thinking, of the old Folio I am reading – & the silence of the silent House is so *most* & very delightful.

This illustrates the "morbid languor of nature, connected both with his fitfulness of purpose and his rich delicate dreaminess" recognised, in Coleridge's work, by Walter Pater. Also, to use Pater's pertinent phrases, the "grievous listlessness" and "physical voluptuousness", and, above all, "that retarding physical burden in [Coleridge's] temperament", are discernible.

As frequently invalided by opium reveries, as by the bowel problems opium was first prescribed for, Coleridge must have been a very depressing man for any 'normal' woman to live with. The following is one example of the many sideswipes that Coleridge would make at Sarah: "The Wife of a man of Genius who sympathizes effectively with her Husband in his habits & feelings is a *rara avis* with me." Coleridge's claims are suspect. Any wife, provoked by the sights of her thin-faced children, outstanding debts, and inert husband, could easily have been forgiven for screaming, *'and how 'most and very delightful' will it be for you when the bailiffs come!'* Kathleen Coburn recalls the caustic humour of Lord Geoffrey Coleridge, when she had asked he, and Lady Coleridge, in the early 30s, for access to the family library at Ottery St Mary:

> 'Old Sam was only a poet, you know, never did anything practical that was any good to anybody, actually not thought much of in the family, a bit of a disgrace in fact, taking drugs and not looking after his wife and children. Of course STC must have been a *wonderful man* – in a way – he was somehow clever enough to take in so many great men – but why a young girl like you should spend your time on the old reprobate, I can't think! All those badly-written scribblings – couldn't even write a decent hand that ordinary people can read – full of stuff and nonsense. But all you pedants *live* on this sort of thing. Useless knowledge, perfectly useless. Now I at least know something about beef cattle ...'

In Lord Coleridge's defence, would the world *be* a better place if everyone's intellectual antennae were tuned into the Coleridgean wavelength? When one is hungry, one is likely to be more interested in a few slices of second-rate topside than STC's choicest metaphysical utterances. But the truth is, we *need* both, and rather more of Coleridge than the moiety we now have.

Perhaps the following notebook entry (1797) is that of a poet who feels that his endeavours have been invisible to those who reserve their praise exclusively for conspicuous utilitarianism: "The picture of a horse sprawling – you have got the wrong way – tis a horse galloping."

He who is outwardly imbecilic inwardly, cuts his way through the trackless jungle of profundity with strength, stamina and skill. His literary productions are all that matter. His lively 'Dotage', as he synthesises what he has assimilated, is transitory. But this is no use to Mrs Coleridge. Not – like Dorothy Wordsworth or Mary Shelley – having been blessed/cursed with such intellectual complications, she needs, first and foremost, financial stability. Coleridge's less visible, more significant, needs have stimulated *him* into such a state of cerebral urgency that neither second, third, nor final reminders about bills to be paid can reel him cleanly out of himself:

> My German Book I have suffered to remain suspended, chiefly because the thoughts which had employed my sleepless nights during my illness were *imperious* over me, & tho' Poverty was staring me in the face, yet I dared behold my Image miniatured in the pupil of her hollow eye, so steadily did I look her in the Face! – for it seemed to me a Suicide of my very soul to divert my attention from Truths so important, which came to me almost as a Revelation/Likewise, I cannot express to you, dear Friend of my heart! – the loathing, which I once or twice felt, when I attempted to write, merely for the Bookseller, without any sense of the moral utility of what I was writing.

Forced by pecuniary concerns to be a hack writer, Coleridge felt himself to be a Pegasus in harness. The fulfilment of his domestic obligations required limitations to his imagination. Southey, whose writing style was, according to Tom Paulin (in *The Day-Star of Liberty: William Hazlitt's Radical Style*, 1998), "uptight and sensuously deprived", much preferred working his way through lists of deadlines, with his imagination tidily shrivelled to the size of a paperweight. When Coleridge did try to attend to the pressures and incentives of the real world, he did so uncomfortably. Naturally, he thought that he needed to disentangle his calling from the confusion of his youthful, domestic, and political anxieties. He was not yet sure what, as a writer, he was supposed to do. He did not consciously *want* to divorce himself from all possible utility. He was, occasionally, nearly suicidal with financial humiliation. But his, as Martin Seymour-Smith (in *Poets Through Their Letters*, 1969) has coined it, "existential inefficiency", was the personal evil whose presence forced the spontaneous contingencies of creativity. It was as if this new, Romantic spirit was finding expression in Coleridge, and, as it was struggling to express itself through him, it was wholly indifferent as to whether or not it was destroying him.

His greatest poems began to arrive, transcending the sprawling mentality out of which they would emerge.

Coleridge and Southey were, for a time occupied with 'Pantisocracy', a project whereby twelve men and their wives would set up a community on the banks of the Susquehanna in the American colonies. (An avalanche of practical difficulties would bury this enterprise.) Just why Coleridge spent so much of his invaluable thinking time with the inferior Southey – and agreed to marry his sister-in-law, Sarah Fricker – is a question that ought to induce weeping. In this context, Hazlitt was right to exclaim, in an essay entitled 'Mr. Coleridge', "Alas! Frailty, thy name is Genius." Even when Southey was plainly failing to practice what he preached (this *"down-right upright republican"* decided after all, amongst other things, that he was going to take a servant with him to America), Coleridge was incapable of telling him that the Pantisocratic enterprise – including Coleridge's impending, loveless, Southey-orchestrated marriage to Sarah Fricker – was off. The following letter to Southey flounders hideously. Here is a mixed-up manner of thinking indeed. It is that of a man hinting frantically to be let off the hook, but never strong enough to risk offending his addressee, by saying what he means:

16

... to marry a woman whom I do *not* love – to degrade her, whom I call my Wife, by making her the Instrument of low Desire – and on the removal of a desultory Appetite, to be perhaps not displeased with her Absence! Enough! These Refinements are the wildering Fires that lead me into Vice. Mark you, Southey! – I *will do my Duty.*

The embarrassing explanation is that Southey was also a father-figure for Coleridge. Coleridge needed his decisions *blessed* in accordance with this ridiculous schema.

However, the two would break. A letter to Poole reveals Coleridge to be taking a more satisfying cognisance of his own comparative vastness as a thinker:

> ... Men of Talents [Coleridge is referring to Southey in this letter] are at present in great request by the Ministry – had I a spark of ambition, I have opportunities enough – but I will be either far greater than all this can end in, even if it should end in my being Minister of State myself, or I will be nothing.

Southey would later review *The Rime of the Ancient Mariner* with the muted bitchiness of the academy:

> Many of the stanzas are laboriously beautiful; but in connection they are absurd or unintelligible ... We do not sufficiently understand the story to analyse it. It is a Dutch attempt at German sublimity.

Now, look at Charles Lamb's response, on Coleridge's behalf, to the malevolent critic:

> I am sorry you are so sparing of praise to the 'Ancient Mariner;' – so far from calling it, as you do, with some wit, but more severity, 'A Dutch Attempt' etc., I call it a right English attempt, and a successful one, to dethrone German sublimity. You have selected a passage fertile in unmeaning miracles, but have passed by some fifty passages, as miraculous as the miracles they celebrate. I never so deeply felt the pathetic as in that part,
>
> > A spring of love gush'd from my heart,
> > And I bless'd them unaware –

It stung me into high pleasure through suffering. [Charles] Lloyd does not like it; his head is too metaphysical, and your taste too correct …

Lamb does here what the hopelessly soft Coleridge was often unable to do for himself. Lamb enforces the Coleridgean sensitivities – demonstrated as they are so strikingly in *The Rime* – with a lightness, yet firmness, of argumentative touch.

There is, however, little point in wishing that Coleridge had had the backbone to send Southey packing and jilt his sister-in-law. Coleridge craved friendship. Then, all is explained. But one could be forgiven for dwelling on the idea that if Coleridge had hardened his heart, he could in the process have lightened it considerably. Had he done so, he would not have suffered, during his most fecund poetic years, a wife who expected him to live his life according to, what was for him, mindless conventionality.

But the thorn of life, as it were, upon which Coleridge fell, and bled the most, was his unrequited passion for Wordsworth's sister-in-law, Sara Hutchinson (who became Coleridge's 'Asra'). Having fallen in love with her at first sight in 1799, Coleridge would spend many years trying to be near her. For instance, he would always be extremely keen for her to act as his amanuensis. She did this often until as late as 1810, on *The Friend*, in the Lake District. It seems that the pressure of the needy poet's company finally forced Sara Hutchinson to move to Wales, to live in her brother's house. Coleridge's pain of longing was very, very slow to heal.

Had it not been for the existence of such raw, emotional nerves in Coleridge (even before he had ever set eyes on 'Asra'), perhaps, he would not have sought solace in opium, and it was opium that gave him the doorway into the unconscious through which he would glean insights that would foreshadow those of Freud and Jung. Coleridge with a 'spine' would not have been Coleridge.

IV   Coleridge and the 'Self'

From 'The Destiny of Nations' (1796), one may infer that Coleridge has started to see himself as being merely the channel for the flow of poetry from beyond the jurisdiction of the conscious poet. The Maid is, like the Mariner to come, animated by some opaque force that is as natural, large and inexorable as the power that pulls the tide. This force, of course, subsumes the individual's own needs and desires:

> And now her flushed tumultuous features shot
> Such strange vivacity, as fires the eye
> Of Misery fancy-crazed! and now once more
> Naked, and void, and fixed, and all within
> The unquiet silence of confused thought
> And shapeless feelings. For a mighty hand
> Was strong upon her, till in the heat of soul
> To the high hill-top tracing back her steps,
> Aside the beacon, up whose smouldered stones
> The tender ivy-trails crept thinly, there,
> Unconscious of the driving element,
> Yea, swallowed up in the ominous dream, she sate
> Ghastly as broad-eyed Slumber! a dim anguish
> Breathed from her look! and still with pant and sob,
> Inly she toiled to flee, and still subdued,
> Felt an inevitable Presence near.

> Thus as she toiled in troublous ecstasy,
> An horror of great darkness wrapt her round,
> And a voice uttered forth unearthly tones,
> Calming her soul ...

Coleridge goes on, enigmatically, yet powerfully, to write of the "gorgeous wings" of "Love" fluttering "Over the abyss ... with such glad noise." The manuscript of this poem contains the following note: "These are very fine Lines, tho' I say it ... but hang me if I know or ever did know the meaning of them, tho' my own composition."

Our familiarity with the idea of the unconscious is a very far cry from the mores of the 1790s. And it was also in an atmosphere where so many personal realities were taboos that Coleridge wrote, and talked, *habitually*, about his personal realities. (In contrast, the majority of Wordsworth's letters (with the exceptions of his passionate love letters to his wife, Mary, in 1812) are guardedly stiff, cold and unfriendly.)

He wrote to Samuel Butler, with whom he studied at university, with a habitual tone of (for the time) intense confessionalism:

> There are hours in which I am inclined to think very meanly
> of myself, but when I call to memory the number & character
> of those who have honoured me with their esteem, I am almost
> reconciled to my follies, and again listen to the whispers of
> self-adulation.

He described his mind on the mend, having recently been divested of its dignity during a vulgar and embarrassing episode that necessitated the financial intervention of his older brother, George Coleridge: "… believe me your severities only wound me as they awake the *Voice within* to speak ah! how more harshly! I feel gratitude and love towards you, even when I shrink and shiver – ". Here, Coleridge, in his early twenties, squirms in the final throes of the Pickwickian pickle he got himself into by joining the 15th Light Dragoons in December 1793. He had assumed a new identity. 'S.T. *Comberbache* [!]' and his far from acquiescent horse would cut many comic profiles, on parades, before the former would be discharged, 'Insane', in April 1794. Whereas, later in the nineteenth century, the Russian novelist and dramatist, Turgenev, in a pseudo-autobiographical short story, would attempt to gloss over his comically exhibited cowardice during a fire at sea, Coleridge did not attempt to excuse or extenuate *his* faults. Instead, he opened his eyes wide to their entire enormity. For Coleridge, to spare the birch as it were, would have been to spoil the truth.

On being offered a generous annuity by Josiah Wedgwood, in 1798, who but Coleridge could have captured, with words, the true slowness with which the spirit of gratitude envelops the human heart? "… my heart has not yet felt any of the swell & glow of personal feelings."

Or again, his unflinchingly honest account of his feelings, and (again) their development, on the birth of his son, Hartley, could scarcely fail to be recognised – no, embraced – by anyone who has ever undergone the strange mental process occasioned by the sudden transition into fatherhood:

> I was quite annihilated by the suddenness of the information
> – and retired to my room to address myself to my Maker –
> but I could only offer up to him the silence of stupified
> Feelings. – I hastened home & Charles Lloyd returned with

me. – When I first saw the Child, I did not feel that thrill & overflowing of affection which I expected – I looked on it with a melancholy gaze – my mind intensely contemplative & my heart only sad. – But when two hours after, I saw it at the bosom of it's Mother; on her arm; and her eye tearful & watching it's little features, then I was thrilled & melted, & gave it the Kiss of a FATHER.

There was just one thing that could have motivated a man, who told countless lies elsewhere in his life, to commit such honesty to paper: a bona fide Miltonic belief in the power of truth to prevail against error. But here lies the Romantic rub in Coleridge. What is truth? John Milton had had the temerity to rewrite Genesis and present it to posterity as *the* definitive explanation for the existence of sin in human beings: *Paradise Lost.* Coleridge, although he strove, in one sense, to emulate Milton, absolutely needed to deal with life's riddle in a hesitant, disconnected, discontented, regretful, capricious, half-mad, never-done-but-always-half-baked way. (An imaginative leap, over the literary output of the Victorians, into modern thought patterns, is required in order to defuse the pejorative charge in these terms and render them terms of commendation.)

Coleridge, according to Leigh Hunt, "not affectedly ... [was possessed by] a high notion of the art in his predecessors." He undoubtedly felt the spirit of the literary greats coursing through his veins. Perhaps opium exposed what lay deep, and dormant, in Coleridge, and that was to subvert his eighteenth-century-conditioned psyche, destroying his happiness with himself, yet ultimately changing English literature beyond recognition.

A letter to his brother, George, on the subject of his lately unwell self now luxuriating in the bodily rewards of recuperation, affords another (small, telling) example of Coleridge's habitual confession-alism: "I am now recovering apace, and enjoy that *newness* of sensation from the fields, the air, & the sun, which make con-valescence almost repay one for disease." Nowadays it is not *so* rare for people to admit the enjoyment they eke out of getting well again after sickness, when not yet well enough to resume the gamut of responsibilities that gives them no time to stand and stare. For a man living in eighteenth century academe, it would have been unheard of.

Like the 16th century French writer, Michel de Montaigne, whose medal was struck with the inscription *Que sçais-je? –* What do I know? – Coleridge examines his own psyche as it reacts to trifles. But when that undiluted Coleridgean morbidity suffuses the senses, the more painful, less gentlemanly self-examination – of the kind yet to be performed by Dostoyevski, in *Notes From Underground* (1864) – sears through the anaesthetic of urbanity. In the early hours of a late-autumn morning, in 1800, a despairing Coleridge heard a noise that he thought might have been his wife in pain, but he also thought that it might have been the wind in the trees. Whatever the source of the sound, it was offering Coleridge the raw echo of his inner desolation:

> Oct. 21 – Morning – 2 o'clock – Wind amid its [?brausen] makes every now & then such a deep moan of pain, that I think it my wife asleep in pain – A trembling Oo! Oo! like a wounded man on a field of battle whose wounds smarted with the cold –

His private confrontation with his wretchedness is characteristically courageous. He acknowledges his far from perfect self:

> My face, unless when animated by immediate eloquence, expresses great Sloth, & great, indeed almost ideotic, good nature. 'Tis a mere carcase of a face:…my gait is awkward, & the walk, & the *Whole man* indicates *indolence capable of energies* … I cannot breathe thro' my nose – so my mouth, with sensual thick lips, is almost always open. In conversation I am impassioned, and oppose what I deem error with an eagerness, which is often mistaken for personal asperity – but I am ever so swallowed up in the *thing*, that I perfectly forget my opponent. Such am I.

It is easy to see how the Maid in 'The Destiny of Nations', herself 'swallowed up in an ominous dream', is really her creator, 'Unconscious of the driving element', yet driven by it further, and more productively, than his contemporaries.

But, more painfully than this, the notebooks would contain the rantings of sexual jealousy, and the embarrassingly theatrical suicide-pacts that Coleridge made with himself: '"Well may I break this

Pact, this League, of Blood/That ties me to myself – and break I shall'". Sometimes, reading Coleridge's notebooks is indulging in the most tasteless eavesdropping. The 1807 entry about his inadvertently finding Wordsworth in bed with the woman for whom Coleridge suffered undying, unrequited love – Sara (more often than not, 'Asra' in the notebooks) Hutchinson – is difficult not to wince at:

> O agony! O the vision of that Saturday morning – of the Bed
> – O cruel! is he not beloved, adored by two – & two such
> Beings. – And must I not be beloved *near* him except as a
> Satellite? – But O mercy, mercy! is he not better, greater,
> more *manly*, & altogether more attractive to any but the purest
> Woman? And yet ... he does not pretend, he does not wish,
> to love you as I love you, Sarah!

Was Wordsworth really the manipulative Lothario who held court, insensitively taking what, and whom, he wanted? It is impossible to ascertain whether or not this scene actually happened. (There is plausible speculation this was an opium induced vision of his worst fear.) But whether or not it was, is beside the point. That is, whatever the mere facts, the truth, as it appeared to Coleridge, about how Coleridge failed to measure up against Wordsworth as a man, is clearly expressed above.

One is inclined to think that there is surely no possibility that Coleridge had a readership in mind, even if a readership of remote posterity, so candid is the man in his (as he would have had it) unpublished secrecy. But there is a declaration, in Notebook 18 – a sort of disclaimer of the permanence of any of the sentiments expressed – which compounds Coleridge's motivation, to be so candid, beyond the neatening touch of the finest tooth-comb of scholarship:

> If I should die without having destroyed this and my other
> Memorandum Books, I trust, that these Hints and first
> Thoughts, often too cogitabilia rather than actual cogitata a
> me, may not be understood as my fixed opinions – but merely
> as the Suggestions of the disquisition; & acts of obedience to
> the apostolic command of Try all things: hold fast that which
> is good.

His brother, George, complained about Coleridge's "specious argumentation". Modern scholars need to be aware of the man's limitless facility in this respect. Like a beloved friend, or family member, Coleridge may, one moment, melt one's heart with his warmth and generosity, and, the next moment, infuriate one with his incurable mendacity.

Coleridge anticipates the work of major 19th and 20th century writers. He reveals his secret morbid psychology and details as the symptoms of his soul challenged by grief, and set apart by spleen. Baudelaire articulated, but published a similar vision in mid 19th century France. Coleridge, however, felt that he could not possibly publish the following, which instead became a notebook entry (1803):

> I write melancholy, always melancholy: You will suspect that it is the fault of my natural Temper. Alas! no. – This is the great Occasion that my Nature is made for Joy – impelling me to Joyance – & I never, never can yield to it. – I am a genuine *Tantalus* –

Baudelaire would trace many of the phases of his own embitterment. Also, he would observe his own ingenuity at self-deception, and his tendency to force his thoughts to cheat each other. He would see clearly how all this rendered his suffering more acute, spoiling in advance, thanks to his powers of analysis and observation, all possibility of happiness.

It is an arresting thought that Coleridge's notebooks, detailing these very symptoms of the modern, alienated mind lay dormant until E.H. Coleridge published a small selection of them, as *Anima Poetae*, in 1895. By then, Baudelaire was long dead, and a twenty-something Marcel Proust was amassing the life experiences with which he would offer his singular guided tour of the byzantine intricacies of memory and desire (*À la Recherche du Temps Perdu*). One may wonder whether or not Proust read the following, from *Anima Poetae*, so remarkably does it encapsulate the Proustian interpretation of life:

> O heavens! when I think how perishable things, how imperishable thoughts seem to be! For what is forgetfulness? Renew the state of affection or bodily feeling (so as to be the)

same or similar, sometimes dimly similar, and, instantly, the trains of forgotten thoughts rise from their living catacombs! [1799]

Oscar Wilde's style was no more flamboyant, nor his conversation more quotable, than Coleridge's. "Melancholy as Sunshine in a dying man's chamber"; "*Outline*/imprisons the mind of the Artist within the first conception/"; "A man who marries for Love a Frog who leaps into a well – he has plenty of water, but he cannot get out again". These quotes lay unseen, for decades between the covers of grubby, inconsequential looking notebooks. Coleridge's vision is wider and more humane than Wilde's.

And think of the eloquence with which Walter Pater (Wilde's mentor) championed the aesthetic of the ecstasy poured, by each moment, into the person living each moment for its own sake. "All our notions husked in the phantasms of Place & Time, that still escape the finest sieve & most searching Winnow of Reason & Abstraction"; "A child scolding a flower in the words in which he had himself been scolded & whipt, is *poetry*/past passion with pleasure". These could be among the resonant bon mots of a Pater treatise. It is perhaps only the inconsistent capitalisation, and the use of obliques (/), that make them identifiable as being parts of a much more private treatise. Coleridge's verbal pliancy could have been as revered as Pater's, or Wilde's, in the post-romantic 'Decadent' era.

Coleridge can speak to the modern age because he is, as he says of Shakespeare, "of no age". By the time Kathleen Coburn was engaged with the task of transcribing and arranging the (still unseen) evidence of Coleridge's importance as a thinker, Camus' novels challenged readers with the fact that *everybody's* personality feels, to each individual, as if it lies around in pieces. In this respect, Coleridge – with his impulse to lay bare his own 'unthinkable' thought patterns – with his willingness to lose his head when all around were keeping theirs – was, in his time, alone.

But that "ache for wholeness" is always present, hovering above the internalised commotion. His 'to do' lists, though never done, do indicate the reality of this august impulse. The fact that he even contemplated writing "a compact compressed History of the Human Mind for the last Century" gives some inkling as to the size of the pot that he expected the heat of his thought to bring to the boil. For the sake of offering another example of a Coleridgean idea, condemned forever to be embryonic, here is an excerpt from a letter to Poole (1801):

> The interval since my last Letter has been filled up by me in the most intense Study. If I do not greatly delude myself, I have not only completely extricated the notions of Time and Space; but have overthrown the doctrine of Necessity. – This I have *done;* but I trust, that I am about to do more – namely, that I shall be able to evolve all the five senses, that is, to deduce them from *one sense*, & to state their growth, & the causes of their difference – & in this evolvement to solve the process of Life & Consciousness.

The exasperation at his own failure to apprehend the totality of spiritual elements – many of which he has himself dreamt into the intellectual universe – sometimes breathes, uneasily, off the page at us: "I cannot write without a *body* of *thought* – hence my *Poetry* is crowded and sweats beneath a heavy burthen of Ideas and Imagery! It has seldom Ease ..."

To put it into perspective, Coleridgean failure is better than the success of many other English writers. Comicality and profundity coexist in Coleridge, just as they do in Chaucer or Shakespeare: " ... I would overwhelm you with an Avalanche of Puns & Conundrums loosened by a sudden thaw from the Alps of my Imagination", he wrote to John Prior Estlin, the Unitarian preacher, and one of Coleridge's patrons.

In the introduction to her small selection of Coleridge's poems and prose (Penguin 1957) Kathleen Raine's anxiety has clearly been occasioned by the harsh obligation: 'What, in such a small selection, should be included, what omitted?'

Some of those contemporary writers who empathised with Coleridge have left behind them valuable sketches of the nature of his creativity:

> Coleridge, like some great river, the Orellana, or the St Lawrence, that, having been checked and fretted by rocks or diverting islands, suddenly recovers its volume of waters, and its mighty music, swept at once ... into a continuous strain of orderly dissertation, certainly the most novel, the most finely

illustrated and traversing the most spacious fields of thought by transitions the most just and logical that it was possible to conceive. What I mean by saying that his transitions were 'just' is by contradistinction to that mode of conversation which courts variety through links of *verbal* connexions. Coleridge, to many people, and often I have heard the complaint, seemed to wander; and he seemed then to wander most when, in fact, his resistance to the wandering instinct was greatest – viz. when the compass and huge circuit by which his illustrations moved travelled farthest into remote regions before they began to revolve. Long before his coming round commenced, most people had lost him.

De Quincey's description, of the scale on which Coleridgean thought unfolds its many parts, and then coheres those parts into the most unaccustomed, prodigious unity, is worth learning by heart. And the following notebook entry (December 1803) reveals Coleridge's grasp of the hierarchy of intellects, and how blindly/seeingly all the gradations of individual perspicuity undergo the human condition, situated in the living universe: "The dim Intellect *sees* an absolute Oneness, the perfectly clear Intellect *knowingly perceives* it. Distinction & Plurality lie in the Betwixt."

This study follows in the understandable tradition of writing about Coleridge, in that it is liberally sprinkled with quotes from his eclectic and soul-searching notebooks and letters. He is, first and foremost, a *vast* thinker with whom the reader must exercise a giant's length of stride to keep apace. He expressed impatience with Lilliputians. He did not suffer "persons troubled with asthma to read" gladly; nor "those … who labour under the more pitiable asthma of a short-witted intellect." But this does not mean that a cursory skim through his dissertations, poems, fragments, etc, will fail to provide the skimmer with an armful of salient observations and treasurable turns of phrase. The reader with the magpie eye will be able to enjoy many fruitful, unsystematic trawls through the Coleridge catalogue. This is at odds with Coleridge's 'aversion to the epigrammatic un-connected periods of the fashionable Anglo-Gallican taste'. The paradox can be explained by the fact that, although he found most readers' "habit of receiving pleasure without any exertion of thought" distasteful, it was not in his nature to banish them from existence. He was gregarious, extrovert and generous. Though he reached its height with ease, he did not live in the ivory tower:

> No real information can be conveyed, no important errors
> rectified, no widely injurious prejudices rooted up, without
> requiring some effort of thought on the part of the reader. But
> the obstinate (and toward a contemporary writer, the
> contemptuous) aversion to all intellectual effort is the mother
> evil of all which I had proposed to war against, the queen bee
> in the hive of our errors and misfortunes, both private and
> national.
>
> (Essay III, *The Friend*, 1809)

Coleridge can be the author of a major cultural complaint without being misanthropic. The tone is, though serious, light. Coleridge is, after all, trying to *sell* his magazine, so he knowingly assumes the rhetoric of easy phrase, but, at the same time, he defames its cankering prevalence in lettered England. This combination is typical.

2 Major Poems

I 'This Lime-Tree Bower My Prison'

The following is from a letter from Coleridge to Southey, 1797:

> Charles Lamb has been with me for a week. He left me Friday
> morning. The second day after Wordsworth came to me, dear
> Sarah accidentally emptied a skillet of boiling milk on my
> foot, which confined me during the whole time of C. Lamb's
> stay and still prevents me from all *walks* longer than a furlong.
> While Wordsworth, his sister, and Charles Lamb were out
> one evening, sitting in the arbour of T. Poole's garden which
> communicates with mine I wrote these lines, with which I am
> pleased ...

The lines with which Coleridge is pleased communicate a strange
deliciousness. It is the (imagined) taste of others' joy at the sights
and sounds of an eagerly anticipated rural walk:

> They, meanwhile,
> Friends, whom I never more may meet again,
> On springy heath, along the hill-top edge
> Wander in gladness, and wind down, perchance,
> To that still roaring dell, of which I told;
> The roaring dell, o'erwooded, narrow, deep,
> And only speckled by the mid-day sun;
> Where its slim trunk and ash from rock to rock
> Flings arching like a bridge; – that branchless ash,
> Unsunn'd and damp, whose few poor yellow leaves
> Ne'er tremble in the gale, yet tremble still,
> Fann'd by the water-fall! and there my friends
> Behold the dark green file of long lank weeds,
> That all at once (a most fantastic sight!)
> Still nod and drip beneath the dripping edge
> Of the blue clay-stone.

These splendidly evoked specifics are on the outskirts of a poetic
vision that is just about to register the tremors of epiphany. The
prospect is then opened out into a more panoramic one; the walkers

have gained a perspective (in the mind of the grounded poet):

> Now, my friends emerge
> Beneath the wide wide Heaven – and view again
> The many-steepled tract magnificent
> Of hilly fields and meadows, and the sea,
> With some fair bark, perhaps, whose sails light up
> The slip of smooth clear blue betwixt two Isles
> Of purple shadow! Yes they wander on
> In gladness all ...

Then Coleridge urges the sun, the flowers, the clouds, the distant groves and the ocean to shine for the benefit of his friends. This Conversation Poem has become radiant with its author's generosity and his wholehearted fideism:

> Ah! slowly sink
> Behind the western ridge, thou glorious Sun!
> Shine in the slant beams of the sinking orb,
> Ye purple heath-flowers! richlier burn, ye clouds!
> Live in the yellow light, ye distant groves!
> And kindle, thou blue Ocean!

These are not the commands of a self-righteous, heavy-handed Prospero, with the elements at his beck and call, and vengeance on his mind. Coleridge, excluded from the walk by circumstances as he has been, wants joy for his friends, not something for himself:

> So my friend
> Struck with deep joy may stand, as I have stood,
> Silent with swimming sense; yea, gazing round
> On the wide landscape, gaze till all doth seem
> Less gross than bodily; and of such hues
> As veil the Almighty Spirit, when yet he makes
> Spirits perceive his presence.

"Silent with swimming sense" suggests mesmerising sensitivity to the crosscurrents of subjective and objective in and around consciousness. Coleridge knows how he himself has felt "On the wide landscape", feeling his self become entangled with his surroundings in the most baffling, and uplifting way. He wants his friends, too, to "gaze till all doth seem/Less gross than bodily".

It is true that this insight's life has been delivered with the pangs of alienation:

> Well, they are gone, and here must I remain,
> This lime-tree bower my prison! I have lost
> Beauties and feelings, such as would have been
> Most sweet to my remembrance even when age
> Had dimm'd mine eyes to blindness! ...

But Coleridge does not luxuriate in lofty solitude, theatrically bewailing his lot as the lone taster of the heavenly banquet of high contemplation. Coleridge is a genuine sharer who has no qualms about sharing with his friends his most insightful ideas.

Coleridge, with the temerity of a gifted twenty-something, has found a way to make hay while the sun (of his inactivity) shines:

> ... Henceforth I shall know
> That Nature ne'er deserts the wise and pure;
> No plot so narrow, be but Nature there,
> No waste so vacant, but may well employ
> Each faculty of sense, and keep the heart
> Awake to Love and Beauty! and sometimes
> 'Tis well to be bereft of promis'd good,
> That we may lift the soul, and contemplate
> With lively joy the joys we cannot share.

As the last two lines of the above excerpt stimulate (rather than argue) us into believing, it is possible to enjoy losing oneself in meditation on an experience that one is not actually experiencing.

Coleridge could decant his harmonising wealth of imagination over any miscellany of thoughts and/or objects. In 'This Lime-Tree Bower My Prison', he orchestrates sublime consonance amid the confusion of unconnected flight paths (of a silently wheeling bat, a swallow, a 'singing' bee, a 'creeking' rook, and planet Earth): "No sound is dissonant which tells of Life."

'This Lime-Tree Bower' is, truly, a *composition*, in that special, musical sense. It is certainly a Conversation Poem, but the feeling of its spiritual significance steadily deepens as it progresses. The poet has primed that serene moment of Understanding. The profound 'bass' of the poem effects an intimation of the fragility of the little things that flutter and buzz so fleetingly in nature. Towards the end of the piece, the bass is lifted into the music of the conversation, modestly proclaiming its quiet, harmonising omnipresence:

> ... not a swallow twitters,
> Yet still the solitary humble-bee
> Sings in the bean-flower!

Years later, in his *Prelude*, Wordsworth would refer to his childhood self as having been a "bee", gathering pleasure from the sights and sounds of the Lake District. It is telling that Coleridge – the pioneer of Conversation Poetry, without whom *The Prelude* could not have been written – presents himself as a *humble*-bee. If Coleridge is a "humble-bee", then 'Kubla Khan' must be a distillation of all the 'nectar' garnered through his meanderings through the 'vast'.

II 'Kubla Khan'

In 1816, it was the un-Romantic Lord Byron who persuaded Coleridge to publish 'Kubla Khan'. Had Byron not done so, the poem may have ended up like, say, Aeschylus' *Myrmidones* – known *about*, but not known. Coleridge had performed 'Kubla Khan' at countless dinner parties, since composing it under the influence of opium, in 1797. Apparently, these performances were absolutely enchanting. However it is only a fragment of a vision.

There is a desire to disbelieve Coleridge's claim that he was interrupted in mid effusion, by "a person on business from Porlock". (Rightly, Richard Holmes believes Coleridge. But it is the unspoken consensus, among academics employed to dispense the received critical wisdom of the moment, that the besotted, romantic, Holmes is in no position to be objective.) Why? Other than the need to not excite comment in professional circles, there is no reason for any reluctance to be seen to appease the Romantic sensibility in this instance. But it seems that postmodern irony prohibits many critics from admitting any validity in even the modest claims of Romanticism.

It is simple. Coleridge's infected intestines were a torture to him. He took, in the literal sense, what the doctor ordered – opium. Directly after an opium-induced sleep, the poet was inspired by his visions.

He immediately set about replicating in words the fully formed thing that he had just glimpsed through a rarely opened door to the unconscious. He found this uncommonly easy to do because he was still in the same room where he had just had the experience, and he had not yet had his mind torn forcibly away. Enter the unsuspecting spoilsport from Porlock.

The imaginative writer is uncomfortably aware of just how tenuous those connections often are between inspiration and execution. If such a connection is damaged, or destroyed, by interruption, its place is too often taken by one palpably lacking its predecessor's organic attachment to the inspiration. This was what could have happened to Coleridge during the writing of 'Kubla Khan'. He could conceivably (as Wordsworth did many times) have sewn many lesser lines throughout the fabric of the vision – bulking it up, out of the skimpiness of a 'psychological curiosity', and into the recognisable proportions of a literary 'masterpiece'. No doubt, a larger, duller 'Kubla Khan' would still have been scintillating. But here, the integrity of true Romantic sensibility – of the kind Coleridge would later say was possessed by Shakespeare – came into its own. Rather than endorse, by practice, the spurious replication of strange, wonderful visions, he presented readers only with those lines fed by the lifeblood of the original inspiration. (How many writers would be able to write at all if they followed the example set by the author of 'Kubla Khan'?) For the excellent reason that it shows the reality of genius, rather than the rhetoric of pretension, here is the fragment in its entirety:

> In Xanadu did Kubla Khan
> A stately pleasure dome decree:
> Where Alph, the sacred river, ran
> Through caverns measureless to man
>   Down to a sunless sea.
> So twice five miles of fertile ground
> With walls and towers were girdled round:
> And there were gardens bright with sinuous rills,
> Where blossomed many an incense-bearing tree;
> And here were forests ancient as the hills,
> Enfolding sunny spots of greenery.

But oh! that deep romantic chasm which slanted
Down the green hill athwart a cedarn cover!
A savage place! as holy and enchanted
As e'er beneath a waning moon was haunted
By woman wailing for her demon lover!
And from this chasm, with ceaseless turmoil seething,
As if this earth in fast thick pants were breathing,
A mighty fountain momently was forced:
Amid whose swift half-intermitted burst
Huge fragments vaulted like rebounding hail,
Or chaffy grain beneath the thresher's flail:
And 'mid these dancing rocks at once and ever
It flung up momently the sacred river.
Five miles meandering with a mazy motion
Through wood and dale the sacred river ran,
Then reached the caverns measureless to man,
And sank in tumult to a lifeless ocean:
And 'mid this tumult Kubla heard from far
Ancestral voices prophesying war!
     The shadow of the dome of pleasure
     Floated midway on the waves;
     Where was heard the mingled measure
     From the fountain and the caves.
It was a miracle of rare device,
A sunny pleasure-dome with caves of ice!

    A damsel with a dulcimer
    In a vision once I saw:
    It was an Abyssinian maid,
    And on her dulcimer she played,
    Singing of Mount Abora.
    Could I revive within me
    Her symphony and song,
    To such a deep delight 'twould win me,
That with music loud and long,
I would build that dome in air,
That sunny dome! those caves of ice!
And all who heard should see them there,
And all should cry, Beware! Beware!
His flashing eyes, his floating hair!
Wave a circle round him thrice,
And close your eyes with holy dread,

For he on honey-dew hath fed,
And drunk the milk of Paradise.

Every syllable of the poem is animated by a preternatural urgency.
The momentum modulates with the untaught, exhilarating control
of a wild animal on the hunt: here (lines 6-11) sinewy, feigned
indifference; there (lines 12-24) awe-inspiringly rapid pursuit through
the undergrowth. 'Kubla Khan' was written because it had to be. It
quickened in, and found its way out of, Coleridge, with an innate,
insatiable craving for a multiplicity of meanings. It has since devoured
readers', and listeners', attentions. And the language still thrives
and struggles with an imperishable rudeness of health and violence
of appetite.

"Could I revive within me/Her symphony and song" says
something that has not yet been said in English literature. With the
help of opium, Coleridge has lowered himself down into his
unexplored depths. On re-ascending, he is excited by the fact that he
has brought some of his darker self back alive, as it were. But he is
disappointed by the fact that he has not brought back much more,
from the strange 'place' where the self and the elements of the living
universe look so puzzlingly entangled from where one normally
stands. He will go down again. And again.

The 'birth' of 'Kubla Khan' was no more the result of the poet's
intellectualism than the birth of a baby is the result of its mother's
intellectualism. The caverns from which the poem comes are
"measureless to man", and therefore measureless to man's intellect.
The last 13 lines effect the whip and snap of the fabric of Coleridge's
humble self pleasurably abandoned in a vast storm of insight. The
poem's naturally occurring music has progressed from something
akin to the dreamy, velvety winding of subtle string and woodwind
instruments (lines 24-27), to the savage pounding of primitive drums
(lines 44-54).

Let us say, for the sake of argument, that the person from Porlock
did, as Coleridge claims, interrupt the flow. It was probably refreshing
for Coleridge to have someone other than his wife rending his thought.
Just think how many Coleridgean works may not have reached us in
the condition they should, because, at crucial points in his negotiations
with the muse, the poet's power of concentration would have been
suddenly flayed and uncreated by ripples of domestic unhappiness:

> ... I am forced to write for bread – write the high flights of poetic enthusiasm, when every minute I am hearing a groan of pain from my Wife – groans, and complaints & sickness! – The present hour, I am in a quickset hedge of embarrassments, and whichever way I turn, a thorn runs into me – . The Future is cloud & thick darkness – Poverty perhaps, and the thin faces of them that want bread looking up to me! – Nor is this all ... I have been composing in the fields this morning ...

This is from a letter to his publisher, Joseph Cottle, in 1796. The suppressed household tension would, before long, become recriminations, and all the inevitable irritations of a shared life would grow poisonous in the hothouse of Mr and Mrs Coleridge's marital incompatibility. A classic, festering mismatch, they quarrelled until the weakest player in the domestic game actually collapsed. (The neediness of opium-addiction combined with her neediness – which manifested itself as her henpecking – became too much for Coleridge.) Then, Sarah suddenly perceived the strong possibility of her husband's imminent death. She mended her ways, but not for her husband's benefit. The following, from a letter of Coleridge's to Southey, effects a flashlight over the secret exigencies of the termagant:

> ... the fears of widowhood came upon her ... these feelings were wholly selfish, yet they made her *serious* – and that was a great point gained – for Mrs Coleridge's mind has very little that is *bad* in it – it is an innocent mind – ; but it is light, and *unimpressible*, warm in anger, cold in sympathy – and in all disputes uniformly *projects* itself *forth* to recriminate, instead of turning itself inward with a silent Self-questioning. Our virtues & our vices are exact antitheses –I so attentively watch my own Nature, that my worst Self-delusion is, a compleat Self-knowledge ... mixed with intellectual complacency ... my quickness and readiness to acknowledge my faults is too often frustrated by the small pain, which the sight of them gives me, & the consequent slowness to amend them. Mrs C ... shelters herself from painful Self-enquiry by angry Recriminations ... Alas! I have suffered more, I think, from the amiable propensities of my nature than from my worst faults & most erroneous Habits ... But as I said – Mrs Coleridge was made *serious* – and for the first time since our

marriage, she felt and acted as beseemed a Wife & a Mother to a Husband, & the Father of her children ...

Coleridge had the intelligence to *see* the science of Sarah's cunning, and articulate it. But it was hard for a poet to use mental energy, better spent elsewhere, sustaining the petty battle campaign. By 1802, Coleridge would feel damaged enough by his marriage to evoke its unhappiness for the benefit of Tom Wedgwood:

> If any woman wanted an exact & copious Recipe, 'How to make a Husband completely miserable', I could furnish her with one – with a Probatum est, tacked to it. – Ill-tempered Speeches sent after me when I went out of the House, ill-tempered Speeches on my return, my friends received with' freezing looks, the least opposition or contradiction occasioning screams of passion, & the sentiments, which I held most base, ostentatiously avowed – all this added to the utter negation of all, which a Husband expects from a Wife – especially, living in retirement – & the consciousness, that I was myself growing a worse man/O dear Sir! no one can tell what I have suffered.

Well, judging by the last sentence, perhaps many more hastily married people than Coleridge realised have 'repented at leisure'.

Really, one should be thankful for the fact that Mrs Coleridge was not as docile and submissive as the wife whom the craftier Southey had picked for himself. The fact that Sarah was so aggressively – even confrontationally – unimaginative meant that Coleridge would *retreat* with increasing regularity. It is clear, from the above excerpt (from the letter to Joseph Cottle), that Coleridge's decision, to compose "in the fields this morning", was not motivated by the desire to self induce Wordsworthian oneness with nature. It was motivated by his need to escape the scornful, desolating remarks, the "freezing looks", and the dispiriting featurelessness of sub-zero matrimony. The shrewish extremes, deployed by Sarah in the private arena of domestic warfare, winkled Coleridge out of any danger of a too comfortable writer's niche. Cervantes was inspired to write *Don Quixote* in a miserable prison. Coleridge was inspired to write 'Kubla Khan' in the quiet of a lonely farmhouse between Porlock and Linton.

Incidentally, nobody knows what 'Kubla Khan' is about. Or rather, like modern physicists on the question of what light is (waves or particles?), any two literary scholars obliged to speak independently may well be expected to offer diametrically opposed theories. Outside the poem's cloud-capped impenetrability, the sound of learned puffing and panting continues today unabated. Scholars have speculatively pinpointed various dates of its composition, and reasons for certain turns of phrase. Yes, Samuel Purchas's *Pilgrimage* (1613), and the books of Milton's *Paradise Lost* set in the Garden of Eden, did amalgamate into a starting point for Coleridge's bizarre psychological incursion. The poem itself is intensely enchanting, but nevertheless continues to evade analysis because it is inexhaustibly suggestive. However, the critic, George Watson, intriguingly, if not convincingly, suggests that "the last paragraph of the poem is a prolonged Platonic allusion", and that "Plato's view of poetic madness" has been the mainspring of Coleridgean thought: as if the "flashing eyes" and "floating hair" in 'Kubla Khan' could be those of the maniacally motivated author of a vague poetic manifesto.

Even though it was composed before the publication of the Wordsworth/Coleridge collaboration, *Lyrical Ballads* (1798), 'Kubla Khan' could not have been comfortably included in a book of narrative poems using 'the real language of men in a state of vivid sensation' (Wordsworth's phrase, in his 1802 Preface to the collection). No, 'Kubla Khan' uses, to put it more accurately, the language of the scientist fired by the raptures of finding himself 'in a world of newly connected and newly modified ideas.' This is a phrase used by Coleridge's great friend, the up-and-coming Cornish chemist, Humphry Davy. Davy is describing an experiment, at which Coleridge was present, involving Davy's imbibing nitrous oxide: "I lost all connection with external things; trains of vivid visible images rapidly passed through my mind and were connected with words in such a manner, as to produce perceptions perfectly novel." Davy was a driven young scientist – the kind whose fearless, obsessive truth-seeking would inspire Mary Shelley to dream up Dr Frankenstein, for her 1818 novel. Davy experimented dangerously, once almost killing himself with carbon monoxide, in his drive to ascertain the effects, on himself, of all sorts of combinations of gasses. Coleridge, too, was more than just a dabbler in all this danger. He was fully conversant with the cutting edge of contemporary science.

In fact, he was part of it, contributing to Davy's *Researches, Chemical and Philosophical; chiefly concerning Nitrous Oxide* (1800).

Kathleen Coburn's 1974 lecture, 'Coleridge: A Bridge between Science and Poetry', deals with the alliance between Coleridge and Davy, and is convincing in its view that Coleridge was as interested in science in a practical sense as he was in theorising about it. Indeed, Coleridge's preface to the 1816 (first) publication of 'Kubla Khan' has something of the flavour of a Davy/Coleridge report on one of the experiments carried out at the Bristol Pneumatic Institute:

> In consequence of a slight indisposition, an anodyne had been prescribed, from the effects of which [I] fell asleep in [my] chair at the moment that [I] was reading the following sentence, or words of the same substance, in *Purchas's Pilgrimage*: 'Here the Khan Kubla commanded a palace to be built, and a stately garden thereunto. And thus ten miles of fertile ground were inclosed with a wall.' [I] continued for about three hours in a profound sleep, at least of the external senses, during which time [I have] the most vivid confidence, that [I] could not have composed less than two to three hundred lines; if that indeed can be called composition in which all the images rose up before [me] as *things*, with a parallel production of the correspondent expressions, without any sensation or consciousness of effort.

He was rare. For Coleridge, the aperture to 'Paradise' could as easily, and suddenly, have opened during his engagement with the gas mask, or with the printed page. And, intellectual giant that he was, he was not precious about clambering, uncouthly, through spontaneous openings on the truth.

'Kubla Khan' is one of the most important poems written in English. In it, Coleridge has his every sinew shaken by a sudden eruption ("momently ... forced") through the familiar crust of his consciousness. His unparalleled accretion of knowledge has bellied out inside him. His subsequently disturbed, subterranean energy vents itself volcanically through the shuffled strata of the opium-dosed Coleridge's word topography.

Until now, it had been the comparatively placid spirit of sensibility that merely dribbled through porous 18th century poetry. Almost every acre of literary England's arable language had been devoted to the cultivation of descriptive specifics. The best poets knew how to ripen classical conventionalities to their optimum vividness. *The Seasons* (1726-30), by James Thomson, and *The Task* (1785), by William Cowper, afford first-rate examples of poetry *aglow* with this confinable sensibility. Indeed, Coleridge's "gardens bright with sinuous rills,/Where blossomed many an incense-bearing tree", seem to suggest that the poet is sitting the reader down, in the first stanza, for the usual, cool, sensible recitation. "But oh!", he exclaims unexpectedly, at the beginning of the second stanza, dropping the preparatory, therapeutic first stanza like a coal suddenly gone hot. There is an immediate increase in the intensity of jostling consonants, and then a fiery flash flood of transfigured words, "with ceaseless turmoil seething". If they are to be recited effectively, lines 17-24 require the skilled performer's energetic best. The *hss*ing, *fss*ing and *thss*ing, and the bumping and pumping of the other consonants, suggests the visceral sensation of unprecedented passage.

Unexpected as it is, Coleridge's revelation is no bolt out of the blue. The percussive tour de force exists to herald the *inevitable* entrance into the intellectual world of something profound. 'Kubla Khan' is not just some old-fashioned dialectic between the old and the new. In Coleridge, the old and the new literary eras collided like continents on the shifting, real world, crushing 'Kubla Khan' up into Himalayan significance.

III *The Rime of the Ancient Mariner*

The Rime (1798) was, like Shakespeare's plays, created with a view to becoming an immediate success and making money. It was written, mostly in the open air, with Wordsworth. The two poets had been casting about for ways and means of finding the money to finance a tour of Germany. 'If only', the two must have thought, 'we could produce something as popular and lucrative as the gothic productions of G.A. Burger and Monk Lewis.' *The Rime* was written with the *Monthly Magazine* firmly in mind.

As Coleridge and Wordsworth trudged over the Quantocks, the expanding and contracting rhythms of their now tramping, now squelching, boots provided the music of the masterpiece. There is no reason, other than the hillwalker's varied intensities of physical exertion as he chaunts poetry into existence, for the stanzas to be sometimes four, sometimes five, and sometimes six lines long. The form of the piece swells and shrinks, with an apparently unpremeditating facility, to accommodate the vicissitudes of the human psyche. With organic, rather than metronomic, regularity, *The Rime of the Ancient Mariner* breathes.

As is often the case with the best lyrics, most of the lines appear unforced. Perhaps the political mud of the day was, loosely, or obliquely, being slung against the wall to see if it would stick. But surely such little, worldly events (that had depressed Coleridge below "*writing-point* in the thermometer of mind") as the 1798 Uprising in Ireland, had nothing to do with his strange, otherworldly tale. Surely *The Rime* was designed to be imbibed by apolitical readers. Well, in England, in the late 1790s, there was no such readership. The critic, Marilyn Butler has remarked that, by 1797, counter-revolutionary hysteria had gained such a grip on England's media that even the word 'philosopher' had become a politically loaded one implying subversion. The fibres of English readers' thought-patterns were highly-strung. It is hard to believe that Coleridge did not know this.

Remember the young radical lecturer's maritime analogy concerning the concept that "everyone ought to consider his intellectual faculties as in a *state of requisition*", as the ship of society has its sails filled by the winds of, and is tossed by the waves of, capricious politics. (*All hands on deck!*) Coleridge may have declared that he has "accordingly snapped [his] squeaking baby-trumpet of sedition", but he is still operating, like the prudent Shakespeare before him, by allegory and implication:

> Listen, Stranger! Storm and Wind,
>   A wind and Tempest strong!
> For days and weeks it play'd us freaks –
>   Like Chaff we drove along.
>
> Listen, Stranger! Mist and Snow,
>   And it grew wond'rous cauld:
> And Ice mast-high came floating by
>   As green as Emerauld.
>
> And thro' the drifts the snowy clifts
>   Did send a dismal sheen;

Ne shapes of men ne beasts we ken –
  The Ice was all between.
The Ice was here, the Ice was there,
  The Ice was all around:
It crack'd and growl'd, and roar'd and howl'd –
  Like noises of a swound.

At length did cross an Albatross,
  Thorough the Fog it came;
And an it were a Christian Soul,
  We hail'd it in God's name.

The Marineres gave it biscuit-worms,
  And round and round it flew:
The Ice did split with a Thunder-fit,
  The Helmsman steer'd us thro'.

And a good south wind sprung up behind,
  The Albatross did follow;
And every day for food or play
  Came to the Marinere's hollo!

In mist or cloud on mast or shroud,
  It perch'd for vespers nine,
Whiles all the night thro' fog smoke-white,
  Glimmer'd the white moon-shine.

'God save thee, ancyent Marinere!
  'From the fiends that plague thee thus –
'Why look'st thou so?' – with my cross bow
  I shot the Albatross.

What are the cracking, growling, roaring and howling noises that surround the ship? The poet and critic, Tom Paulin, has suggested that the din generated by the ice is symbolic of Revolution, and, in particular, Coleridge's split feelings on the subject. On one hand, Coleridge is a violently committed Jacobinical Republican. On the other, he believes wholeheartedly in the sacral nature of the monarchy. So, when the Mariner shoots the albatross with his crossbow, he is violently going against the sacral nature of the monarchy. Isn't Coleridge sublimating the political dimensions of the day, leaving only the apolitical tip of the iceberg visible?

Wordsworth's *Prelude* would later contain exactly the same brand of politically resonant sound effects. For example, there is a passage in *The Prelude* that recollects an episode in Wordsworth's childhood (1780s pre-Revolutionary Europe):

> ... Meanwhile abroad
> Incessant rain was falling, or the frost
> Raged bitterly, with keen and silent tooth;
> And, interrupting oft that eager game,
> From under Esthwaite's splitting fields of ice
> The pent-up air, struggling to free itself,
> Gave out to meadow-grounds and hills a loud
> Protracted yelling, like the noise of wolves
> Howling in troops along the Bothnic Main.

Irish antennae are finely tuned to receive the most furtive signals, transmitted by Seamus Heaney's poetry, concerning political violence, and the torn, guilty psyche that craves justice *and* peace. Similarly, where Coleridge's 1798 *Rime* is concerned, violence and guilt are examined, not on the bloodsoaked streets of Paris, but in strange latitudes.

In *Areopagitica* (1644), which famously attacked government censorship of the press, John Milton had asked: "Who shall silence all the airs and madrigals that whisper softness in chambers?" It could be argued that the author of *The Rime* is a thoroughly political animal with the intuition(?) canniness(?) to chew the political fat in a context less damaging to his personal prospects. After all, he took his anonymous political journalism in the *Courier* very seriously indeed. Rupert Christiansen offers an appetite-whetting encomium regarding this:

> ... reading his paragraphs now, it is impossible not to admire
> his grasp of the issues, the height of his moral perspectives,
> and his ability to see, without smugness, the virtues of both
> the progressive and conservative positions. He detested
> Napoleon, and was forced to accept the idea of a 'necessary
> war' against him – but he never [like Wordsworth] lost either
> his pity for the victims of a ruthless social order or his anger
> against the oppressors. Unlike the politicians around him, he

managed to refuse expedients, stand firm on Christian principles, and yet remain sharp-eyed and realistic.

Chapter XXII of the *Biographia Literaria* steadily becomes a welter of enthusiasm on the subject of Wordsworth's poetry. Coleridge points the reading public in the direction of particularly beautiful passages from 'Intimations of Immortality' and 'The White Doe'. Coleridge's admiration for the poetry of his former collaborator is indicated, as the chapter progresses, by the increasing length at which he quotes from it, and the decreasing sense of the necessity of his critical intervention. It is as if Coleridge, at the beginning of the chapter, holds his reader balanced on the two-wheeled simplicity of Wordsworthianism. The reader is held tight for a while, like a child, learning to ride a grown-up's bicycle, being given the time, love and support to develop a feel for the unnerving lack of complication. Soon, even as the reader's handling of the Wordsworthian vehicle is closely superintended, the Coleridgean stabilisers are almost imperceptibly removed by their progenitor – the loving, unthanked father who, having let go, watches cultural England pedal towards the light of (*Wordsworthian*) refinement, growth and development.

It is time Coleridge was quoted with a similar minimum of place-hunting, academic fuss. The following passage, from *The Rime*, speaks for itself:

> I saw a something in the Sky
>   No bigger than my fist;
> ' At first it seem'd a little speck
>   And then it seem'd a mist:
> It mov'd and mov'd, and took at last
>   A certain shape, I wist.
>
> A speck, a mist, a shape, I wist!
>   And still it ner'd and ner'd;
> And, an it dodg'd a water-sprite,
>   It plung'd and tack'd and veer'd.
> With throat unslack'd, with black lips bak'd
>   Ne could we laugh, ne wail:
> Then while thro' drouth all dumb they stood
> I bit my arm and suck'd the blood
>   And cry'd, A sail! a sail!

With throat unslack'd, with black lips bak'd
　　Agape they hear'd me call:
Gramercy! they for joy did grin
And all at once their breath drew in
　　As they were drinking all.

She doth not tack from side to side –
　　Hither to work us weal
Withouten wind, withouten tide
　　She steddies with upright keel.

The western wave was all a flame,
　　The day was well nigh done!
Almost upon the western wave
　　Rested the broad bright Sun;
When that strange shape drove suddenly
　　Betwixt us and the Sun.

(Notice, just above, how the intensity of the imagined experience thaws the necessity out of any shallow desire to find some different word to rhyme with 'Sun'.)

And strait the Sun was fleck'd with bars
　　(Heaven's mother send us grace)
As if thro' a dungeon grate he peer'd
　　With broad and burning face.

Perhaps a Quantock sun, glimpsed through the happenstance arrangement of trees' leafless branches, provided Coleridge with an external specific to transliterate into his vision. But then the vision, as it gets closer still, sharpens into the unmistakable clarity of inner, inchoate fears realised:

Alas! (thought I, and my heart beat loud)
　　How fast she neres and neres!
Are those *her* Sails that glance in the Sun
　　Like restless gossameres?

Are those *her* naked ribs, which fleck'd
　　The sun that did behind them peer?
And are those two all, all the crew,
　　That woman and her fleshless Pheere?

> *His* bones were black with many a crack,
>   All black and bare, I ween;
> Jet-black and bare, save where with rust
> Of mouldy damps and charnel crust
>   They're patch'd with purple and green.
>
> *Her* lips are red, *her* looks are free,
>   *Her* locks are yellow as gold:
> Her skin is as white as leprosy,
> And she is far liker Death than he;
>   Her flesh makes the still air cold.

"She" is a ghastly spirit half conjured up out of the reader by the somnambular, feverish word association of *lips, looks, locks*. The reader reluctantly is reminded that there is an unchallengeable authority about one's unexamined, irrational fears, once they have been summoned. "She" *speaks*:

> The naked Hulk alongside came
>   And the Twain were playing dice;
> 'The Game is done! I've won, I've won!'
>   Quoth she, and whistled thrice.

"He" is less articulate, but just as eloquent:

> A gust of wind sterte up behind
>   And whistled thro' his bones;
> Thro' the holes of his eyes and the holes of his mouth
>   Half-whistles and half-groans.

This is followed by the deaths of the two hundred crew members. It is all the Mariner's fault. He should not have shot the albatross. He is further dismayed by the discovery that he is unable to pray:

> I look'd to Heav'n, and try'd to pray;
>   But or ever a prayer had gusht,
> A wicked whisper came and made
>   My heart as dry as dust.

This brings the predicament of Hamlet's stepfather/uncle to mind, who found himself unable to pray, having just been traumatised anew by the fact that he had murdered Hamlet's real father: "My words fly up, my thoughts remain below,/Words without thoughts never to Heaven go." (III, iii).

Coleridge's imagination appears to have been sparked by the horror of Jacobean drama. Look at how something prevents the guilty Mariner from not looking at the consequences of his own sin:

> I clos'd my lids and kept them close
>   Till the balls like pulses beat;
> For the sky and the sea, and the sea and the sky
> Lay like a load on my weary eye,
>   And the dead were at my feet.
> The cold sweat melted from their limbs,
>   Ne rot, ne reek did they;
> The look with which they look'd on me,
>   Had never pass'd away.
>
> An orphan's curse would drag to Hell
>   A spirit from on high:
> But O! more horrible than that
>   Is the curse in a dead man's eye!
> Seven days, seven nights I saw that curse,
>   And yet I could not die.

In Tourneur's macabre ballet, *The Revenger's Tragedy* (1607), the disguised brothers, Vindice and Hippolito, trick the (sinful) Duke into kissing a skull. They then force him, at knife-point, to watch, in silence, from the shadows, his wife and bastard son cursing him, and kissing each other, in pre-copulatory excitement (III, v). Like Tourneur's Duke, Coleridge's Mariner desperately wants to die immediately, but is obliged to endure what he sees. Being forced, in whatever way, to look at the evidence of the (inevitable human) error of one's ways, held a deep fascination for Coleridge. He wrote about the guilty conscience, in 1798, to his brother, George. George was, by then, intimately knowledgeable regarding precisely what it was that troubled Coleridge in this way:

> I believe most steadfastly in original Sin; that from our mothers' wombs our understandings are darkened; and even where our understandings are in the Light, that our

47

organization is depraved, & our volitions imperfect; and we sometimes see the good without *wishing* to attain it, and oftener *wish* it without the energy that wills and performs.

Coleridge knew himself. "Metaphysics make all one's thoughts equally corrosive on the Body by the habit of making momently & common thought the subjects of uncommon interest and intellectual energy." This December 1802 notebook entry shows the great thinker's awareness of the sacrifices, and dangers, involved in living for the fire that burns inside. He did not let himself off the hook. Nor did he let others off his hook. In this sense, the Mariner is Coleridge. Outwardly, he cuts that musty, dowdy, down at heel profile recognised so quickly, and avoided with such dexterity, by 'normal' people who just want to have a good time. After all, the wedding-guest is just on his way in to the gathering of friends and relatives, at least some of whom may have in mind his expected presence. Who, in these circumstances, would willingly allow himself to be accosted by a complete stranger?

It is an ancyent Marinere,
　And he stoppeth one of three:
'By thy long grey beard and thy glittering eye
　'Now wherefore stoppest me?
'The Bridegroom's doors are open'd wide,
　'And I am next of kin;
'The Guests are met, the Feast is set, –
　'May'st hear the merry din.
But still he holds the wedding-guest –
　There was a Ship, quoth he –
'Nay, if thou'st got a laughsome tale,
　'Marinere! come with me.'
He holds him with his skinny hand,
　Quoth he, there was a ship –
'Now get thee hence, thou grey-beard Loon!
　'Or my Staff shall make thee skip.

Strange sufferings have harrowed the Mariner's features and gait out of the readily acceptable mould of cheery amenability that one must display at weddings. The initially repellent intensity of the Mariner is due to the fact that he aggressively offers a most unwelcome bridge from frivolity to profundity – from the wedding-guest's frivolity to *his* profundity. Initially, the intrusion has an almost comically futile impertinence.

Coleridge is fully aware of the awkwardness, embarrassment and hostility elicited by inappropriately urgent thought. But the Mariner, hypnotically, "holds [the wedding-guest] with his glittering eye", and "hath his will". There then follows the most astonishing sequence of recollected events, punctuated occasionally by the wedding-guest's exclamations of fear and wonder.

The Rime is thick-strewn with the kind of assonance, onomatopoeia and alliteration that conduced to the poetic achievement of Edmund Spenser's *Faerie Queene* (1590-96). Coleridge would later lecture admiringly on the technique of the Elizabethan poet from whom he had learned so much:

> You cannot read a page of the *Faerie Queene*, if you read for
> that purpose, without perceiving the intentional alliterativeness
> of the words; and yet so skilfully is this managed, that it never
> strikes any unwarned ear as artificial, or other than the result
> of the necessary movement of the verse.

Coleridge's deep and serious study of the old master's style influenced *The Rime*. Perhaps never before, or since, had assonance been deployed to this effect: "Alone, alone, all all alone/Alone on the wide wide Sea". The doleful tolling of the ghostly vowels, in this line, somehow communicates a sense of unforgettably total isolation. Whatever it is that haunts the language of this poem, not one puff of its ghastliness has been exorcised during the poem's march into the realm of cultural clichés. Coleridge has exploited the power in repetition to its full potential:

> Day after day, day after day,
>   We stuck, ne breath ne motion,
> As idle as a painted Ship
>   Upon a Painted Ocean.
>
> Water, water, every where,
>   And all the boards did shrink;
> Water, water, everywhere,
>   Ne any drop to drink.

> The very deeps did rot: O Christ!
>   That ever this should be!
> Yea slimy things did crawl with legs
>   Upon the slimy Sea.

The repetitive, and the nearly repetitive, sound patterns come and go like the cloud formations one may have witnessed gathering and dispersing in time-lapse photography. They are addictive for no apparent reason.

By the end of the poem, the Mariner has not just succeeded in detaining the wedding-guest for the best part of half an hour: he has changed his life. The question, "What manner man art thou?" draws the following direct utterance from the Mariner, his language still electrified by the nervous energy brought into being by his ordeal:

> Forthwith this frame of mine was wrench'd
>   With a woeful agony,
> Which forc'd me to begin my tale
>   And then it left me free.
>
> Since then at an uncertain hour,
>   Now oftimes and now fewer,
> That anguish comes and makes me tell
>   My ghastly aventure.

The attack of the language, bouncing rhythmically, is offset by the mesmerising, yet succinct, metaphors that suffuse the piece with an unimpeachable aura of serenity, and sublimity:

> I pass like night, from land to land;
>   I have strange power of speech;
> The moment that his face I see
> I know the man that must hear me;
>   To him my tale I teach.

One looks at the phrase, "I pass like night", and one recognises its author as an exquisitely intuitive angler who fishes words from strange seas of thought, alone. The "I ... night" comparison is startlingly reeled into clear view, wriggling with life, but remains untranslatable and unparaphraseable. This is Romanticism at its inchoate, yet unfogged, best. Again, Coleridge's great enthusiasm about Spenser is probably connected with this peculiar aspect of the poetic success of *The Rime*:

> Observe also the exceeding vividness of Spenser's descriptions. They are not, in the true sense of the word, picturesque; but are composed of a wondrous series of images, as in our dreams ... You will take especial note of the marvellous independence and true imaginative absence of all particular space or time in the *Faerie Queene*. It is in the domains neither of history or geography; it is ignorant of all artificial boundary, all material obstacles; it is truly in land of Faery, that is, of mental space. The poet has placed you in a dream, a charmed sleep, and you neither wish, nor have the power, to inquire where you are, or how you got there. It reminds me of some lines of my own ...

But the question of how Coleridge got that full, oceanic swell, into the troublesome personal waters so forcefully suggested by *The Rime*, could scarcely be explained by his relationship with Spenser's work.

To understand the poem, one must realise that Coleridge has experienced the voyage, about which he writes – on the 'sea' of matrimony. Practically pressed, by Robert Southey, into marrying Sarah Fricker, the earnest young Coleridge did enjoy the ceremony and honeymoon. Mr and Mrs Coleridge set sail, so to speak, in a blaze of untried optimism:

> The Ship was cheer'd, the Harbour clear'd –
>   Merrily did we drop
> Below the Kirk, below the Hill,
>   Below the Light-house top.

For a short time after marriage, the sun went "Higher and higher every day", and shone pleasantly on the newlywed Coleridges. Then, the inevitable tempestuousness of a young couple held sway:

> For days and weeks it play'd us freaks –
> Like Chaff we drove along.

After this, Sarah's recriminatory coldness engulfed the household as the three, including their first-born son, Hartley, tried to live off Coleridge's irregular earnings. Straitened circumstances close one in, and when things are like this for months – even years – there may be the nauseating feeling in family life that something is just about to give:

> The Ice was here, the Ice was there,
> > The Ice was all around:
> It crack'd and growl'd, and roar'd and howl'd –
> > Like noises of a swound.

Fate came to the rescue, offering to steer the Coleridges free of their mounting money worries. Coleridge was offered the comfortably salaried post of Unitarian minister at Shrewsbury, with a good family house to live in as well:

> At length did cross an Albatross,
> > Thorough the Fog it came ...

Surely – Sarah must have thought – Samuel will treat this piece of good fortune with the necessary tact, and take the job that will save our family from more penury! Won't he? The Albatross gives the Coleridge crew/family a little taste of how a regular wage, at long last, would break down so many barriers:

> And an it were a Christian Soul,
> > We hail'd it in God's name.

> The Marineres gave it biscuit-worms,
> > And round and round it flew:
> The Ice did split with a Thunder-fit,
> > The Helmsman steer'd us thro'.

> And a good south wind sprung up behind,
> > The Albatross did follow ...

Coleridge sees the opportunity of a permanent post. He could hardly fail to see it. It has flown right through the fog and moonshine of his endless – and financially unreliable – reading, scribbling and dreaming, and "perch'd" itself in front of he and his family in no uncertain terms:

> In mist or cloud on mast or shroud,
> > It perch'd for vespers nine,

> Whiles all the night thro' fog smoke-white,
> Glimmer'd the white moon-shine.

Southey would not have 'slain' such a creature (career opportunity) in his wildest dreams. Coleridge would be left with nothing but his wildest dreams if he rejected the offer of security for his family. He must have known that even gently-spoken failure to take his family's financial matters in hand would have brought him unbearable isolation, and face to face dealings with unspeakably awful personal demons. (Sarah would become irreconcilably bitter with him, and it would be distinctly possible that he would live the rest of his life with the painful awareness that he had not provided for his own children.) But Coleridge's rejection of comforts from heaven was instinctive and violent. Without a shudder, he took aim and fired: "I shot the Albatross."

So, the career opportunity was obliterated. Without the steady wind of a regular wage in their sails, the Coleridges were soon 'becalmed':

> Down dropt the breeze, the Sails dropt down,
> 'Twas sad as sad could be
> And we did speak only to break
> The silence of the Sea.

Coleridge had to endure the isolation that Guilt brings:

> Ah wel-a-day! what evil looks
> Had I from old and young;
> Instead of the Cross the Albatross
> About my neck was hung.

Condemned by his own earlier choice to shoot the Albatross, the protagonist sees ghastly visions unseen by the rest of the crew/family. The dead crew looks at the Mariner with curses for him on their faces. Looking through the door of his undoing, the Mariner sees the sentiments, of those he has let down, from inside his blackened imagination. Coleridge has found a device to communicate how it feels – in his disastrous marriage – to suffer hostile attention, and yet suffer it in solitary confinement!

Coleridge undergoes penance until he meets Wordsworth. Who

else could the serene Hermit be but the Wordsworth we know to have daily emanated the piety of common sense, and composed his more comfortably imagined visions? The "Mariner" quickly throws himself at the feet of someone who he believes will lead him to a promised land of wholesomeness, sobriety and sanity:

> I saw a third – I heard his voice:
>   It is the Hermit good!
> He singeth loud his godly hymns
>   That he makes in the wood.
> He'll shrieve my soul, he'll wash away
>   The Albatross's blood.

The Mariner begs: "'O shrieve me, shrieve me, holy Man!'"
    Having suffered acute alienation, Coleridge yearns for friendship:

> … this soul hath been
>   Alone on a wide wide sea:
> So lonely 'twas, that God himself
>   Scarce seemed there to be.
> O sweeter than the Marriage-feast,
>   'Tis sweeter far to me
> To walk together to the Kirk
>   With a goodly company.

Coleridge yearns for love. But, in his experience, this yearning became a *thirst* upon a sea of ill-starred matrimony: "Water, water, every where,/Ne any drop to drink." The prolonged absence of drinking water, with only the salt spray to taste, has driven unlucky seafarers mad. The prolonged absence of love, with Sarah Fricker moodily appearing on deck from time to time, may explain the recurrent opening out, and closing in, of the "Mariner's" lyrical eloquence. Coleridge's poetry *cries*. Later, in 'The Pains of Sleep' (1803), Coleridge would state, with heartrendingly childlike simplicity: "To be beloved is all I need". He felt that he was not 'beloved'. Feeling abandoned like this somehow liberated him to roam the labyrinths of his personal Hell. The strange gifts, with which he returned from those awful sojourns, would be received by the second generation of English Romantic poets. If one looks at 'The Eve of Saint Agnes', by Keats, or 'Hymn to Intellectual Beauty', by

Shelley, one easily sees that familiarly undimmable, *Coleridgean* lustre.

The protracted exertion and consuming self-control that enabled Coleridge to write poetry as great as *The Rime* would take its toll on him. There is a letter to Tom Poole (January 1801) in which Coleridge explains away his responsibility, as a genius, to operate at full tilt:

> As soon as my poor Head can endure the intellectual & mechanical part of composition, I must immediately *finish* a volume which has been long due – this will cost me a month, for I must not attempt to work hard.

Having repeatedly alluded to his weakness, or dizziness, Coleridge finishes the letter with: " – I have scarce strength left to fold up the letter –". Somewhat theatrically, Coleridge was carefully informing each of his friends and acquaintances not to expect any more works of genius from him. Having continually sensed people's bated breath in expectation of his next masterpiece, he set about systematically debunking his own poetic prowess in an effort to rid himself of the chains of their hopes around him.

Great writers have had praise lavished on them. Having written the epic poem, *Paradise Lost*, in 1665, Milton must have had his ego feathered with the warm approval of at least one contemporary in order to be able to sit down to compose (unfortunately) *Paradise Regained* that same year. Coleridge – the purveyor of provisional shards, flints and fragments – had anticipation, not praise, lavished on him. (Thomas Talfourd was still lavishing anticipation on Coleridge in 1815, in *The Pamphleteer*: "Little as Mr Coleridge has written, he has manifested not only a depth but a variety of genius, from which the most brilliant results might be expected ...") So, his fecund genius yielded much of what has since come to be perceived as problematic prose and poetry. In the hall of literary fame, where Milton's celebrated achievement is unambiguously beribboned, Coleridge's name is garlanded with thornier flowers.

IV 'Christabel'

> But through her brain of weal and woe
> So many thoughts moved to and fro,
> That vain it were her lids to close;
> So half-way from the bed she rose,
> And on her elbow did recline
> To look at the lady Geraldine.

True enough, 'Christabel' would never be finished. It hangs luminously like the dream whose events cannot be properly recalled to memory. Any potential for narrative development melts away in the face of what David Punter (in *The Romantic Unconscious*, 1989) has called the "chronic intrusion of the inexplicable".

However, what there would come to be of 'Christabel' would greatly inspire John Keats to write 'The Eve of Saint Agnes' (1820) – one of his finest poems. It would also inspire Byron and Scott. The fact that Coleridge failed to publish what he managed to write of 'Christabel' until 1816 gave Scott and Byron their opportunity to use, for their own works, what they had privately seen of it. By the time Coleridge published 'Christabel', it would have appeared that he was merely recycling the ideas of Byron and Scott! So, in the Preface, Coleridge pre-emptively offered "this doggerel version of two monkish Latin hexameters", in an attempt to playfully disarm any lurking critics:

> 'Tis mine and it is likewise yours;
> But an if this will not do;
> Let it be mine, good friend! for I
> Am the poorer of the two.

It may be diluted into magnanimity by his sweet gentility, but Coleridge's gentle mockery is evident. It is worth quoting a sentence, from the same Preface, which encapsulates just how rare true poetry is, and therefore how the true poet has the devil's own job convincing people that s/he is an original:

> For there is amongst us a set of critics, who seem to hold, that
> every possible thought and image is traditional; who have no
> notion that there are such things as fountains in the world,

small as well as great; and who would therefore charitably
derive every rill they behold flowing, from a perforation made
in some other man's tank.

There is a sort of naturally occurring, out-of-focus, dream-dipped
radiance about the first part of 'Christabel'. The second part does
not have this. For all Coleridge's technical mastery of the apparatus
with which Spenser concocted dreamscapes, it was never going to
be easy for Coleridge (having relaxed the sinews of his mind out of
this once-in-a-lifetime state) to re-establish the precise combination
of imaginative elements that facilitated the original magic blur.
Having absented himself from the pressure of continuing with the
second part of the poem, Coleridge must, on returning to the task,
have found it impossible to fuse the constituent parts of his
imagination back into 'Christabel'-mode. It would have been the
poetic equivalent of trying to un-stir a cup of coffee.

Christabel discovers Geraldine in the moonlit wood. Geraldine,
it seems, has been kidnapped:

> Five warriors seized me yestermorn,
> Me, even me, a maid forlorn:
> They choked my cries with force and fright,
> And tied me on a palfrey white.

But the momentum of the narrative rarely progresses for long before
becoming translucent with liquefyingly nebulous meaning:

> The palfrey was as fleet as wind,
> And they rode furiously behind.
> They spurred amain, their steeds were white;
> And once we crossed the shade of night.
> As sure as Heaven shall rescue me,
> I have no thought what men they be;
> Nor do I know how long it is
> (For I have lain entranced I wis)
> Since one, the tallest of the five,
> Took me from the palfrey's back,
> A weary woman, scarce alive.
> Some muttered words his comrades spoke:
> He placed me underneath this oak;
> He swore they would return with haste;

Whither they went I cannot tell –
I thought I heard, some minutes past,
Sounds as of a castle bell.
Stretch forth thy hand (thus ended she),
And help a wretched maid to flee.

There is the obvious implication that the reader is to forego the pleasure of unambiguous narrative. The flashes of light are at their most effective in the gloomy recesses of obscure, yet suggestive, passages.

There is still dramatic tension in the midst of all the vagueness. The following captures the visual specific of Christabel's feet, stealing up a staircase, reflecting alternating light and shade with almost supernatural rapidity, in an atmosphere mentally charged with the energy of troubled stealth:

Sweet Christabel her feet doth bare,
And jealous of the listening air
They steal their way from stair to stair,
Now in glimmer, and now in gloom,
And now they pass the Baron's room,
As still as death, with stifled breath!
And now have reached her chamber door;
And now doth Geraldine press down
The rushes of the chamber floor.

By now, the reader is immersed in the bewitching lake of Coleridge's imagination:

The moon shines dim in the open air,
And not a moonbeam enters here.
But they without its light can see
The chamber carved so curiously,
Carved with figures strange and sweet,
All made out of the carver's brain,
For a lady's chamber meet:
The lamp with twofold silver chain
Is fastened to an angel's feet.

One is to bathe, fascinated, in the Romantic ambience of this, rather than swim hurriedly across it to get to the 'How?', 'Why?', or

'Conclusion' – those comfortable narrative garments that readers often expect the author to have draped, in easy view, on the far shore of the story.

For Hazlitt, among other critics, this would never do:

> In parts of 'Christabel' there is a great deal of beauty, both of thought, imagery, and versification; but the effect of the general story is dim, obscure, and visionary. It is more like a dream than reality. The mind, in reading it, is spell-bound. The sorceress seems to act without power – 'Christabel' to yield without resistance. The faculties are thrown into a state of metaphysical suspense and theoretical imbecility.

The critic, Karen Swann, with her characteristic psychoanalytic insight, writes more perceptively about Coleridge's motivation. She selects contemporaneous notebook entries that show that Coleridge was inspired to compose the poem by "the vertiginous play of objects and representations, inside and outside, and even of perception, speculation, and sensation." The discrepancies, between the mind's picture of a thing and the actual, objective thing, are the wellsprings that nourish the peculiarity of the vision. Swann is much more satisfyingly alert than Hazlitt regarding this reflective dimension: "For as Coleridge's attempts to grasp the scene result in its oscillation between warring interpretive possibilities, the scene itself comes to represent a queasy [sensation]…"

His inability to complete 'Christabel' became one of his guilty obsessions. A very brief notebook entry, in 1801, would at first appear to succinctly account for the failure: "Into a *discoverer* I have sunk from an *inventor!*" But the word "sunk" says – in Coleridge-speak – it all. By this stage he had developed a certain philosophical detachment about his poetic failure. Look at the earlier attempt by Coleridge to account for his inability to complete 'Christabel'. Hope is fading, but it is not yet dead. (Wordsworth has yet to realise his full manipulative potential and reject the poem, in December, for inclusion in the second edition of *Lyrical Ballads*.) It is November 1800:

> … immediately on my arrival in this country I undertook to finish a poem which I had begun, entitled 'Christabel', for a second volume of the *Lyrical Ballads*. I tried to perform my

promise; but the deep unutterable Disgust, which I had suffered in the translation of that accursed Wallenstein seemed to have stricken me with barrenness – for I tried & tried & nothing would come of it. I desisted with a deeper dejection than I am willing to remember ...

So, Schiller's *Wallenstein*, the sustained contemplation of which had intrigued Coleridge in the direction of some of his finest Romantic insights – including those into Shakespeare – was getting the blame. Before Wordsworth's obtuse decree ("upon mature deliberation", that 'Christabel' "was so discordant from my own [style] that it could not be printed along with my poems with any propriety"), Coleridge was being optimistic. Hence, the sense in the above excerpt, from his letter to Josiah Wedgwood, that he was trying to keep his poet's ego afloat, clutching at the flotsam of excuses.

Surely the "sacred river" of Coleridgean originality cannot meet the great, uncharted sea of philosophical problems without major whirlpools foundering the poet and quickly afterwards depositing him on the nearest shoreline: "... I hope, Philosophy & Poetry will not ... leave me an inert mass." These are the words of a poet/ philosopher fearful of losing his way.

The following December 1803 notebook entry shows Coleridge privately cutting to the root of his inability to finish works, such as 'Christabel':

> The Soul within the Body, can I any way compare this to the Reflection of the Fire seen thro' my window on the solid Wall, seeming of course within the solid wall, as deep within as the distance of the Fire from the Wall? – I fear, I can make nothing out of it/ but why do I always turn away from any interesting Thought to do something uninteresting – as for instance, when this Thought struck me, I turned off my attention suddenly, & went to look for the Wolff which I had missed – /Is it a cowardice of all deep Feeling, even tho' pleasurable? or is it Laziness? or is it some thing less obvious than either? – Is it connected with my epistolary Embarrassments?

Indeed. Has even the most tenaciously single-minded poet, philosopher, or scientist, never been plagued by an inability to sustain objectivity for more than a paltry few moments? Whilst intent on achieving great things, writers and thinkers take their frequent breaks by indulging in 'unworthy' mental intricacies. Indolence is one of the most important components of the creative faculty. One cannot, in one's personal depths, continually confront one's own limitations without coming up for air. The student possessing the melancholy knowledge of how long it took to complete the last essay is invariably able to measure out the struggle in coffee spoons and cigarettes. In this respect, Coleridge is a genius with whose opinions the common reader is often glad to concur. This is part of what makes him so attractive. His intellect was clearly a noble one, yet he was not at all without that salty admixture of approachability. He was an unassuming, multi-faceted genius.

In his old age, Coleridge had refined a charismatic, though questionable, insouciance about personal failure. The following extract, from *Table Talk* (July 1833) demonstrates this:

> The reason of my not finishing 'Christabel' is not, that I don't know how to do it – for I have, as I always had, the whole plan entire from beginning to end in my mind; but I fear I could not carry on with equal success the execution of the idea, an extremely subtle and difficult one. Besides, after this continuation of *Faust*, which they tell me is very poor, who can have courage to attempt a reversal of the judgement of all criticism against continuations?

He is like the magician at a children's party talking his way out of the fact that there are no more rabbits to be magically produced from his hat. But Coleridge could see this about himself too. Only a sentimental sense of obligation could prevent party-goers from ejecting their silly, boring old uncle:

> Like some poor nigh-related guest,
> That may not rudely be dismist;
> Yet hath outstay'd his welcome while,
> And tells the jest without the smile.

This, from a later poem ('Youth and Age', 1823-32), shows that there was no recess of self-respect into which the writer's self-harrowing omniscience could retire.

V   'Frost At Midnight'

Coleridge does something very strange in 'Frost At Midnight' (1798). Inviting the reader into the holiest recess of Coleridge's silence, the poet has discovered the crackle of electricity that connects his waywardly thinking brain with Everything:

> 'Tis calm indeed! so calm, that it disturbs
> And vexes meditation with its strange
> And extreme silentness. Sea, hill, and wood,
> This populous village. Sea, and hill, and wood,
> All the numberless goings-on of life,
> Inaudible as dreams! the thin blue flame
> Lies on my low-burnt fire, and quivers not;
> Only that film, which fluttered on the grate,
> Still flutters there, the sole unquiet thing.
> Methinks, its motion in this hush of nature
> Gives it dim sympathies with me who live,
> Making it a companionable form.
> Whose puny flaps and freaks the idling Spirit
> By its own moods interprets, every where
> Echo or mirror seeking of itself,
> And makes a toy of Thought.

However much a toy can be made of Thought, these are not, as Dr Johnson famously complained of 17th century metaphysical poets' efforts, "heterogeneous ideas yoked by violence together".

The way Coleridge plays with *his* mental toys is not at all aggressive. The tenuity of the concept in 'Frost At Midnight' is undisguised. The only point of connection between the "Sea, hill, and wood" with the "low-burnt fire" is in the poet's brain. And no intellectual bullying attempts to enforce like-mindedness in the reader. With Coleridge, there is never the sense, anywhere in the mind of the reader as s/he reads, of a peremptorily forced parade of ideas. Intellectually, Coleridge has a giant's strength, but he does not use it like a giant. Coleridge conducts his ideas to the threshold of the reader's mind, and then just lets them infiltrate like the suggested sound of bells, in 'Frost At Midnight' – capable of activating a thousand different trains of thought in a thousand different minds.

'Frost At Midnight' is a poem from which one of Coleridge's

most intense bursts of "antediluvian" (to use De Quincey's word) sensitivity washes out into subsequent imaginative literature, such as Wordsworth's *Prelude*:

> The Frost performs its secret ministry,
> Unhelped by any wind. The owlet's cry
> Came loud – and hark, again! loud as before.
> The inmates of my cottage, all at rest,
> Have left me to that solitude, which suits
> Abstruser musings: save that at my side
> My cradled infant slumbers peacefully.

It is probable that it is opium that has modulated Coleridge's consciousness into a tinglingly sensitive, radiating plasma. He now enjoys, his mental faculties' "most exquisite order, legislation, and harmony" (to use De Quincey's words). The film of soot that flutters on the grate is taken from the section of William Cowper's *The Task* that evokes a wintry evening spent in a firelit drawing room. But, as the "sooty films ... play upon the bars", Cowper's "understanding takes repose/In indolent vacuity of thought,/And sleeps ...". With each flap of the film in *Coleridge's* poem, "in this hush of nature", opium-kissed ripples of heightened awareness expand their concentric circles through time and space, re-including Everything in this opulent vision, with minimum explanation:

> But O! how oft,
> How oft, at school, with most believing mind,
> Presageful, have I gazed upon the bars,
> To watch that fluttering *stranger*! and as oft
> With unclosed lids, already had I dreamt
> Of my sweet birth-place, and the old church-tower,
> Whose bells, the poor man's only music, rang
> From morn to evening, all the hot Fair-day,
> So sweetly, that they stirred and haunted me
> With a wild pleasure, falling on mine ear
> Most like articulate sounds of things to come!
> So gazed I, till the soothing things, I dreamt,
> Lulled me to sleep, and sleep prolonged my dreams!
> And so I brooded all the following morn,
> Awed by the stern preceptor's face, mine eye
> Fixed with mock study on my swimming book:

Save if the door half opened, and I snatched
A hasty glance, and still my heart leaped up,
For still I hoped to see the *stranger's* face,
Townsman, or aunt, or sister more beloved,
My play-mate when we both were clothed alike!

The silence in the house is pregnant with preternatural energy. The presence of this energy is thrown into relief by the "gentle breathings", of Coleridge's infant son, that "Fill up the interspersed vacancies/And momentary pauses of the thought!"

This poem was conceived in a *quality* silence – the kind of silence that has absolutely nothing to do with loneliness, or emptiness; the kind of silence that actually empowers the consciousness. Modern readers should be able to respond to this. There is something significant there for each us to read in the grain of his/her unpolished solitariness:

> ... so shalt thou see and hear
> The lovely shapes and sounds intelligible
> Of that eternal language, which thy God
> Utters, who from eternity doth teach
> Himself in all, and all things in himself.
> Great universal Teacher! he shall mould
> Thy spirit, and by giving make it ask.

The conclusion of this poem contains exquisite little individual images: of a robin redbreast garlanded with snowy branches, and a thatched roof having the remains of the night's freeze steamed off it by the rising sun. But the total effect amounts to much more than what Coleridge called Cowper's "divine chit chat". Amazingly, for a so-called 'conversation poem', ripples of energy harmonise the "goings-on of life,/Inaudible as dreams", into a liquid totality. This, in turn, is gorgeously frozen into a jewel of a poem.

With his professed constitutional indifference to the praise or censure of contemporaries, Coleridge hangs 'Frost At Midnight' up to shine, 'Quietly', to posterity.

VI 'Dejection: An Ode'

'Dejection: An Ode' (1802) is the product of the vilest, blackest depression. One does not need to be psychologically incapacitated by dependence on any drug to understand what Coleridge is saying in this poem. Sufferers from depression – whether mild or acute – will discern the validity of every word of the following:

> A grief without a pang, void, dark, and drear,
>   A stifled, drowsy, unimpassioned grief,
>   Which finds no natural outlet, no relief,
>   In word, or sigh, or tear –

There is perhaps only one other example, in all literature, of this particular mode of misery being so well expressed:

> ... O God! God!
> How weary, stale, flat and unprofitable
> Seem to me all the uses of this world! [*Hamlet* I, ii]

Truly debilitating depression may prevent one, not only from doing one's work, but from doing *anything*. In Coleridge's case, he finds himself unable to convert what he perceives of the external world into poetry:

> ... in this wan and heartless mood,
> To other thoughts by yonder throstle woo'd,
>   All this long eve, so balmy and serene,
> Have I been gazing on the western sky,
>   And its peculiar tint of yellow green:
> And still I gaze – and with how blank an eye!

One problem for Coleridge was that Wordsworth was by now (1802) in very fine poetic fettle. Whereas Coleridge believed himself to be flummoxed in the unpublishable mire of his own decrepitude, Wordsworth's *Resolution and Independence* (1802) was densely populated with readable, entertaining natural scenery:

> But now the sun is rising calm and bright;
> The birds are singing in the distant woods;
> Over his own sweet voice the Stock-dove broods;

The Jay makes answer as the Magpie chatters;
And all the air is filled with pleasant noise of waters.

The subject of Wordsworth's poem was depression – *and how to beat it*. And in Wordsworth's 'Intimations of Immortality' ode (1802), the poet takes Dante's lead and makes the stalwart decision not to be sullen in the sweet air:

Oh evil day! if I were sullen
While Earth herself is adorning,
  This sweet May-morning,
And the Children are culling
  On every side,
In a thousand valleys far and wide,
Fresh flowers; while the sun shines warm ...

But it is easy to make the decision not to be depressed when you are not depressed. Even today, people who do not suffer from depression are often inclined to wonder, incredulously, why sufferers don't just redouble their efforts and get on with things.

With all the prejudices engendered by his own state of well-being, Wordsworth has confined himself, as a poet, to exploring the mere surface of the soul. He does not penetrate any of the darker recesses unless they are easily accessible, and calmly lit with the candles of Christian precepts. Wordsworth's only concern seems to be with *healthy* virtues and vices. 'Steer clear of morbidity!' he tells readers. 'If morbidity does get you, snap out of it!'

People wanted to read this kind of advice then, and they still do now. There have been many, many books published, offering already healthy, robust readers sound, practical pep talks. Their underlying message is simple: don't be weak. Those who aspire to stride through life, preceded by the great, fiery cross of Positive Thinking, will require indomitably genial spirits.

But what about the rest of us? Intellectually, Wordsworth is offering the sufferer let's say, of a chronic back problem, the equivalent of an exercise manual. Coleridge is not so impertinent. Coleridge tells the truth:

My genial spirits fail;
And what can these avail

To lift the smothering weight from off my breast?
It were a vain endeavour,
Though I should gaze for ever
On that green light that lingers in the west:
I may not hope from outward forms to win
The passion and the life whose fountains are within.

Stanza 6 recounts, with the power of almost magically condensed autobiography, how it came to this pass:

There was a time when, though my path was rough,
This joy within me dallied with distress,
And all misfortunes were but as the stuff
Whence Fancy made me dreams of happiness:
For hope grew round me, like the twining vine,
And fruits, and foliage, not my own, seemed mine.
But now afflictions bow me down to earth:
Nor care I that they rob me of my mirth;
But oh! each visitation
Suspends what nature gave me at my birth,
My shaping spirit of Imagination.
For not to think of what I needs must feel,
But to be still and patient, all I can;
And haply by abstruse research to steal
From my own nature all the natural man –
This was my sole resource, my only plan:
Till that which suits a part infects the whole,
And now is almost grown the habit of my soul.

Coleridge admires Wordsworth as by far the greatest of the modern poets. But Coleridge's sensibilities are more discernibly attuned to the tensions rippling outwards, on deep psychological trouble, from Shakespeare's Hamlet:

I have of late – but wherefore I know not – lost all my mirth,
forgone all custom of exercises, and indeed it goes so heavily
with my disposition that this goodly frame, the earth, seems
to me a sterile promontory. This most excellent canopy, the
air, look you, this brave o'erhanging firmament, this majestical
roof fretted with golden fire, why, it appears no other thing to
me than a foul and pestilent congregation of vapours.

[*Hamlet* II, ii]

For Coleridge in 'Dejection', as for Hamlet, the individual, subjective consciousness has been clarified in the fullness of depression, the mind has gone flat, and the bouquet of geniality has evaporated. There is nothing either good or bad but thinking makes it so:

> And those thin clouds above, in flakes and bars,
> That give away their motion to the stars;
> Those stars, that glide behind them or between,
> Now sparkling, now bedimmed, but always seen:
> Yon crescent Moon, as fixed as if it grew
> In its own cloudless, starless lake of blue;
> I see them all so excellently fair,
> I see, not feel, how beautiful they are!

The almost physical heaviness, of whose company there is no riddance for Coleridge as he tries to compose, is formulated beautifully in the following letter (to William Sotheby, 1802):

> I wished to force myself out of metaphysical trains of thought, which, when I wished to write a poem, beat up game of far other kind. Instead of a covey of poetic partridges with whirring wings of music, or wild ducks *shaping* their rapid flight in forms always regular (a still better image of verse), up came a metaphysical bustard, urging its slow, heavy, laborious, earth-skimming flight over dreary and level wastes... For I believe that by nature I have more of the poet in me. In a poem written during that dejection, to Wordsworth, and the greater part of a private nature, I thus expressed the thought in language more forcible than harmonious.

VII   'The Delinquent Travellers'

> Some are home-sick – some two or three,
> Their third year on the Arctic Sea –
> Brave Captain Lyon tells us so –
> Spite of those charming Esquimaux.
> But O, what scores are sick of Home,
> Agog for Paris or for Rome!
> Nay! tho' contented to abide,
> You should prefer your own fireside;
> Yet since grim War has ceased its madding,

And peace has set John Bull agadding,
'Twould such a vulgar taste betray,
For very shame you must away!
'What? not yet seen the coast of France!
The folks will swear, for lack of bail,
You've spent your last five years in jail!'

In 1824, Coleridge would write the extremely wry, witty and
accurately observed 'Delinquent Travellers'. This poem debunks the
widely (and almost religiously) embraced belief that it is necessary,
interesting and useful to travel abroad. "'Tis now the rage,/The law
and fashion of the Age." Kant never left Königsberg, but this fact
did nothing to stop him effecting a paradigm-shift. A man's spiritual
well-being, Coleridge knows as well as Wordsworth, lies no more
in travel than it does in champagne and oysters. This wisdom is
timeless. Just as a gourmet menu writer's efforts at arousing the
salivations of an undiscriminating palate are wasted, so a 19th century
Baedeker's precise, laconic details are unable to stir the contents of
an empty English head. Coleridge had always been inclined to make
fun of the inability of commonplace people "to comprehend who
labour under the ... pitiable asthma of a short-witted intellect." Now
(in 1824) that Coleridge considers himself no longer to be a great
poet, his liberated, mischievous lightness of verse, applied to the
subject of the lack of spiritual ballast in the modern Englishman,
complements Wordsworth's rather more insistent austerity
concerning that subject. Coleridge, whose best poetry has been the
record of his alienation, now becomes "one of the lads", ironically:

Receive me, lads! I'll go with you,
Hunt the black swan and kangaroo,
And that New Holland we'll presume
Old England with some elbow room.

In his feigned eagerness to achieve the globe-trotter's credentials
that make fashionable the curriculum vitae of the (otherwise
commonplace) Englishman, Coleridge is comically disingenuous:

And if there's nought left to explore,
Yet while your well-greased wheels keep spinning,
The traveller's honoured name you're winning.

The idea of continental travel, in lieu of the finishing school veneer, which distinguishes men with the *bon ton* for the society in which they intend to shine, excites the derision of Coleridge, as much as it does the disdain of Wordsworth. In 'The Delinquent Travellers', the flippancy with which Coleridge flicks stereotypical picture-postcard sketches into the reader's view effects a racy satire of all the shallowness, restlessness and affectation that gives rise to delinquent itinerancy. For Coleridge, most 1820s travellers seek to cram their memories with experiences of, "those charming Esquimaux", or that "numerous band/of cockneys [that] anglicise the strand" at Boulogne. For Coleridge, these memories are useless in themselves. It is the power of Coleridge's mind, *habituated to the Vast* as it is, that animates such dead matter:

> Move, or be moved – there's no protection,
> Our Mother Earth has ta'en the infection –
> (That rogue Copernicus, 'tis said
> First put the whirring in her head,)
> A planet She, and can't endure
> T'exist without her annual Tour:
> The *name* were else a mere misnomer,
> Since Planet is but Greek for *Roamer*.

With its obvious echoes of *The Rime*, a torrent of travel-related images flows down the page.

The contempt for shallowness is lightly worn, and what would, in other hands, have become aggressively clattering syllables, in Coleridge's, become unwarlike battalions of otherworldly sparks and flashes that are entirely under his command:

> Across the mountains we will roam,
> And each man make himself a home:
> Or, if old habits ne'er forsaking,
> Like clock-work of the Devil's making,
> Ourselves inveterate rogues should be,
> We'll have a virtuous progeny;
> And on the dunghill of our vices
> Raise human pine-apples and spices.

This is a performance poem. The 'Mariner' (Coleridge) reciting it is attractively wry, rather than repellently cynical. There is no brandished calendar of personal regrets. There is no bitterness. There are no polemics. Yet there are still unmistakable traces of mistakes having been made, battles having been fought, life having been lived:

> Of all the children of John Bull
> With empty heads and bellies full,
> Who ramble East, West, North and South,
> With leaky purse and open mouth,
> In search of varieties exotic
> The usefullest and most patriotic,
> And merriest, too, believe me, Sirs!
> Are your Delinquent Travellers!

3   Gossip and Art

Great musicians must practice for hours every day, in order to be physically able to reach a high level of attainment and experession. Similarly, painters must paint. And writers must write. But, Coleridge had to *talk*. In this respect, he did not behave in the way the genius is supposed to. He did not exclusively hone his writing skills in the supposed, Wordsworthian seclusion. Nor did he endure critical neglect before eventually emerging into posterity to receive the long-awaited laurel of genius. No, Coleridge was admired, *and* criticised, as he grew, in public. As a young man, he preached many Unitarian sermons, delivered radical lectures, and threw himself into close relationships with people who would each be taken aback by the intensity involved in being Coleridge's friend. Poole, Southey and Wordsworth would all experience the demands made on the intellect, imagination, and patience, by such a remarkable man.

The early 19th century was an era in which intellectuals rounded each other's corners down in conversation. Philosophical ideas were floated, and sunk, in the combative straits bordering their progenitors. This was long before the existential age, during which it would become fashionable for lone philosophers to fire their ideas up into the godless void like gloriously futile distress signals. Coleridge was 'of his time' in that he rarely conducted misanthropic monologues. Instead, he empathised with his interlocutors, as one intoxicated, empathises with one's similarly intoxicated cohorts: "Two drunken men, arm in arm, the one imagining himself sober, the other acknowledging himself drunk, the former *acting* the other's leader & care-taker." This June 1800 notebook entry suggests that Coleridge thought metaphysical 'clarity' to be as achievable through words as 'sobriety' is through drink.

And so it was that Coleridge evolved out of the morbid intolerance for human error that other great thinkers – such as the extremely influential Arthur Schopenhauer – developed in isolation from society. Some of the older Coleridge's writings, reflecting on the (unmerited) arrogance of his younger self, foreshadow the melancholic narrative of Dickens' older 'Pip' recollecting some of the less flattering traits of his younger self, in *Great Expectations* (1850):

> Before I was eight years old, I was a *character* – sensibility, imagination, vanity, sloth, & feelings of deep and bitter contempt for almost all who traversed the orbit of my understanding, were even then prominent and manifest.

One only has to look at Chapter 2 of the *Biographia Literaria*, on the "Supposed irritability of men of genius", to fully realise how uninterested Coleridge is in cutting the profile of the easily annoyed inhabitant of a higher mental plane. In this, Coleridge suggests Thomas Love Peacock. Mr Hilary, in Peacock's shrewdly sensitive novel, *Nightmare Abbey* (1818), discusses contemporary attitudes to poets' legendary grumpiness, and counters the fashionably endemic depression:

> We have sufficient proofs on record that Shakespeare and Socrates were the most festive of companions. But now the little wisdom and genius we have seem to be entering into a conspiracy against cheerfulness.

In this novel, there is even mention of a maternal ancestor of the main character, Scythrop, "who hanged himself one rainy day in a fit of *tedium vitae*". It soon came to be understood, satirically speaking, that aspiring poets were to be misanthropic, exhibit suicidal despondency, and intrigue onlookers while at the same time disdaining them. Only in notebook secrecy (1819) would Coleridge allow himself to mould the genuinely antisocial impulses in him into art:

> Robb'd, jilted, slander'd, poor, without a hope,
> How can I chuse but be a Misanthrope?

It is very significant that two voices – Wordsworth's and Coleridge's – talked *The Rime of the Ancient Mariner* into existence. It is equally significant that Coleridge talked his essays for *The Friend* into existence, dictating his developing ideas to Asra; and he used John Morgan as his amanuensis for the delivery of the *Biographia Literaria*. His frequent conversations with William and Dorothy

Wordsworth led to the Preface of *Lyrical Ballads*, which is one of the most penetrating critiques of English culture ever written.

Clement Carlyon, a Fellow of Pembroke College and friend of Coleridge, recounts Coleridge's endless talking, on a walking tour in Germany, in 1799. It was with a party of highly intelligent young men, and when words were needed to describe something indescribable, guess who produced the metaphysician's clear-eyed catch of the day?

> When we were ascending the Brocken, and ever and anon stopping to take breath, as well as survey the magnificent scene, a long discussion took place on the sublime and beautiful. We had much of Burke, but more of Coleridge ... Many were the fruitless attempts made to define sublimity satisfactorily, when Coleridge, at length, pronounced it to consist in a suspension of the powers of comparison.

It is perhaps something of a minor, cultural injustice that Coleridge's pronouncement on the sublime did not become as famous as his explanation that theatre-goers need to exercise a "willing suspension of disbelief" at any given play, in order to help make the play work.

People who knew Coleridge wanted to be with him because his incessant talk ensured the frequent unearthing of new treasures. Just as the agility of an acrobat is betrayed by a rare elasticity in his ordinary movements as well as in his performed ones, so it was an instructive pleasure to witness a supple intellect even as it negotiated commonplaces. Coleridge was aware of this, and wrote (or rather, *said* to Asra, for her to write) about it for Essay IV of *The Friend*:

> What is that first strikes us, and strikes us at once, in a man of education; and which among educated men so instantly distinguishes the man of superior mind, that (as was observed with eminent propriety of the late Edmund Burke) 'we cannot stand under the same archway during a shower of rain, without finding him out'? Not the weight or novelty of his remarks; not any unusual interest of facts communicated by him; for we may suppose both the one and the other precluded by the shortness of our intercourse and the triviality of the subjects. The difference will be impressed and felt, though the conversation should be confined to the state of the weather or

the pavement. Still less will it arise from any peculiarity in his words and phrases.

So, what is it that distinguishes the superior mind? Not surprisingly, this is among the many conceptual nails that Coleridge hits sweetly on the head with his journeyman's tool – his conversation, and his conversational style of writing:

> It is the unpremeditated and evidently habitual arrangement of his words, grounded on the habit of foreseeing in each integral part, or (more plainly) in every sentence, the whole that he then intends to communicate. However irregular and desultory his talk, there is method in the fragments.

Coleridge is, of course, writing about himself. The conversation of a superior mind may seem pointlessly fragmentary to an inferior participant lacking the mental dexterity to retain the separate elements of a concept, for synergy later on. Coleridge was, insofar as a vast thinker can be, a modest man; and there are no accolades for modesty in the literary bear garden. But he is clearly writing his own encomium here:

> [commonplace minds] at once divide and announce the silent and otherwise indistinguishable lapse of time. But the man of methodical industry and honourable pursuits does more; he realizes its ideal divisions, and gives a character and individuality to its moments. If the idle are described as killing time, he may be justly said to call it into life and moral being, while he makes it the distinct object not only of the consciousness but of the conscience. He organizes the hours and gives them a soul; and that, the very essence of which is to fleet away, and evermore to have been, he takes up into his own permanence, and communicates to it the imperishableness of a spiritual nature.

The German pessimistic philosopher, Arthur Schopenhauer, without whom Nietzsche, Wagner, Proust, Freud, Camus, Thomas Hardy, Wittgenstein and Mahler would not have had their common starting point, seems to have imbibed Coleridge's wisdom wholesale:

[commonplace] people make this shallow, empty and troubled existence an end in itself. To the life of the intellect such a man will give the preference over all his other occupations: by the constant growth of insight and knowledge, this intellectual life, like a slowly-forming work of art, will acquire a consistency, a permanent intensity, a unity which becomes ever more and more complete; compared with which, a life devoted to the attainment of personal comfort, a life that may broaden indeed, but can never be deepened, make but a poor show: and yet, as I have said, people make this baser sort of existence an end in itself.

Schopenhauer is Coleridge, minus God, plus gloomy, gloating satisfaction. His contempt for mediocrity feverishly makes its presence heard as the unintelligent monotone, while he works it out of his system.

He sounds this same note so many times in his essays from the *Parerga And Paralipomena* (1851) that (inspirational and consoling as his writing has undoubtedly been to lofty, malcontent souls everywhere) he must have been attacking something in himself. Yet Coleridge has everything offered by Schopenhauer, except the posturing reductionism. In a way, Schopenhauer is Coleridge for nihilists:

If this world were peopled by really thinking beings, it could never be that noise of every kind would be allowed such generous limits ... If Nature had meant man to think, she would not have given him ears; or at any rate, she would have furnished them with air tight flaps, such as are the enviable possession of the bat. But, in truth, man is a poor animal like the rest, and his powers are meant only to maintain him in the struggle for existence; so he must needs keep his ears always open, to announce of themselves, by night as by day, the approach of the pursuer.

At least Coleridge does not constantly remind us that we are merely poor, bare, forked animals, and laugh at us in this affectedly demonic way. But, more significantly, at least Coleridge came first. It was he who mingled at Göttingen University, winnowed his (and others') ideas in lively conversations, and committed the distillation of (his and those of German philosophers, past and contemporary) ideas to paper. He endured crippling unhappiness as an opium-addict, but did not stew in his own foul air with the view that his readers ought to be grateful for the stench. No,

> He organizes the hours and gives them a soul [This, unlike Schopenhauer's Olympian misanthropy, bears repeating] … Of the good and faithful servant, whose energies, thus directed, are thus methodized, it is less truly affirmed that he lives in time, than that time lives in him. His days, months, and years, as the stops and punctual marks in the records of duties performed, will survive the wreck of worlds, and remain extant when time itself shall be no more.

In 1803, Coleridge made a note in his notebook to "Get [some works of] *Chamfort*". Nicholas Chamfort (1741-94) was a French miscellaneous writer whose brilliant conversation, power of sarcasm, and epigrammatic force, coupled with an extraordinary career, rendered him one of the most interesting and remarkable men of his time. Schopenhauer undoubtedly owed much to this writer, to whom he constantly referred. Schopenhauer made striking bouquets out of the already flowered cynicism of talents, like Chamfort, who had made to entertain readers with his contemptuous take on the falsehood, hollowness and hypocrisy of human affairs. But, as Schopenhauer himself said in his essay, 'On Style', "Style is the physiognomy of the mind, and a safer index to character than the face." It is true that Schopenhauer's "physiognomy" is as terminally deformed with self-importance as some of the charlatans he so detests. After a while the bitter voice of the outsider, challenging the norms of in-grown philosophy departments, looses its delectable polemical edge.

Coleridge's ability to compel unalloyed assent is hampered by no Schopenhauerian distaste at human error. After all, human error is so necessary, paradoxically, to intellectual exchange. Shouldn't participants in a conversation be allowed to take their inevitable (yet often illuminating) wrong turns? The stoic silence of the genius in a folly-ridden world may well signal a valiant attempt to protect a little pocket of mental purity from contamination brought about by social intercourse with a dullard. But one soon craves (even if against one's 'better' judgment) the kind of silly flamboyance that Coleridge recognised in Chaucer. In short, the enclosed, mental celibacy of Wordsworth's "plain living and high thinking" was not for Coleridge. Intellectual promiscuity, not to mention glasses of punch, at the 'Salutation & Cat' was more congenial to him. In the spring of 1796, he holidayed for two weeks at Tom Poole's Stowey home. Much poetry was recited, and much local cider was consumed, in Poole's garden. The monastic discipline shown by Kant (in accordance with whose ultra-precise regularity of daily habits many Königsberg residents set their watches!) would have been counter-productive for the Coleridge's temperament. He told Southey that:

> I have been the slave of Impulse, the Child of Imbecility –
> But my inconsistencies have given me a tarditude & reluctance
> to think ill of any one – having been often suspected of wrong,
> when I was altogether right, from *fellow-feeling* I judge not
> too hastily from appearances. Your undeviating Simplicity
> of Rectitude has made you too rapid in decision – having
> never erred, you feel more *indignation* at Error, than *Pity* for it.

The airless void of space is not at all congenial to conversation. Air is the essential medium for the voice. For Coleridge, as a matter of comparable urgency, the interpersonal space, between the speaker and the spoken to, must be made crossable by the media of love and compassion. Otherwise, the transmission of wisdom is impaired, or even destroyed. It ought to be remembered that, in Coleridge's words, "little is taught or communicated by contest or dispute, but every thing by sympathy and love". In *In Pursuit of Coleridge*, Kathleen Coburn remembers Gertrude Boyle, one time indexer of the notebooks:

> One day when I was driving her home in a thick blizzard
> through slow traffic that gave opportunity for ample talk,
> [Gertrude] made a characteristically honest confession of the
> softening influence of STC on her. In reporting someone's
> misfortunes or mistakes or unhappiness of some kind, she
> said, 'Well, it's really all her own fault ...' and then stopped
> herself short. 'Oh, no,' she said, 'that's not true'. With a
> sheepish smile she turned to look me in the eye. 'Thanks to
> Mr Coleridge I don't think in that way anymore.'

In a letter to Thomas Allsop (December 1818), Coleridge waxes melancholically on the subject of his formerly intense alliance with the Wordsworth family, and, in particular, on the sympathy-shaped hole in the Wordsworthian methodology:

> ... I have loved with enthusiastic self-oblivion those who have been so well pleased that I should, year after year, flow with a hundred nameless Rills into *their* Main Stream, that they could find nothing but cold praise and effective discourage-ment of every attempt of mine to roll onward in a distinct current of my own – who *admitted* that the 'Ancient Mariner', the 'Christabel', the *Remorse*, and *some* pages of the 'Friend' were not without merit, but were abundantly anxious to acquit their judgements of any blindness to the very numerous defects. Yet they *knew* that to *Praise*, as mere Praise, I was characteristically, almost constitutionally indifferent. In Sympathy alone I found at once Nourishment and Stimulus: and for Sympathy alone did my heart crave ...

So, with his conversation, and conversational style of writing, Coleridge often strove to fill up the interpersonal void by tickling up the love and compassion in his reader/listener. He told Tom Poole that "the notion of a Soul is a comfortable one to a poor fellow, who is beginning to be ashamed of his Body." Part genuine, part calculated, self-effacement like this primes Poole's attentiveness. If Coleridge did practice the arts of the beggar, he refined them way beyond recognition. Richard Holmes has said, concisely, about Coleridge's letters, that each was "characteristically tailored to its recipient." Humphry Davy's attentiveness is primed, in the following example, not so much with self-effacement as with an enjoyably absurd *body politic* analogy:

> ... A Rheumatic Fever sentenced me to the Bed-bastille ... a most excruc[ia]ting pain on the least motion, but not without motion, playing Robespierre & Marat in my left Hip & the small of my back ...

Coleridge knew that he could do something useful to the face made stern by studious habits and earnest truth seeking. He could make it smile every so often. Cerebral benefits accrue from the sudden relaxation of *one-way* effort. Coleridge knew that health-promoting properties are released, by humour, into any tightened mentality as it reads. Then, that mentality, pleasurably athrob with the unexpected propulsion of sudden ease, will be more inclined to reciprocate – not least by helping Coleridge in some material way.

Coleridge had the emotional capacity to house the huge torsions brought about by unaffected engagement with genuine philosophical problems. The shifting fabric of Coleridge's intense and subtly analysed thought glistens with the complexities of his mind and personality. It glistens in a way that makes Schopenhauer – that great and influential scorner of professional weaklings – seem like a purveyor of fruitlessly detached philosophising. The works of Schopenhauer, and those of the great authors influenced by his irascible genius, are very often enjoyed in the effluvium of the reader's self-regard. Not one to deny the presence of contradictory thoughts, Coleridge admitted such a predilection in himself, as well as admitting his need for moral support:

> ... much as I loathe flattery from the bottom of my very *stomach*, and much as I *wriggle* under the burden and discomfort of the praise of people, for whose heads, hearts, and specific competence I have small respect, yet I own myself no self-subsisting mind. I know, I feel, that I am weak, apt to faint away, inwardly self-deserted, and bereft of the confidence in my own powers; and that the approbation and sympathy of good and intelligent men is my sea-breeze, without which I should languish from morn to evening, – a very trade-wind to me, in which my bark drives on regularly and lightly ...

In this letter to Sir George Beaumont (February 1804), Coleridge characteristically articulates, during a characteristic digression, the driving, and eddying, elements of his inner, intellectual *weather-conditions*. The fact that such an important philosophical thinker owns himself "no self-subsisting mind ... weak ... [and] inwardly self-deserted" is, at the very least, a stimulating change for those of us who may otherwise be too easily bewitched by some or other illusion of intellectual self-containment.

It is invigorating to be able to reach back through the 20th and 19th centuries – and make contact with Coleridge. A notebook entry, made by Coleridge (winter, 1801), makes clear his comprehension of his own intellectual/imaginative independence from any past Chamforts or future Schopenhauers:

> Some flatter themselves that they abhor egotism – & do not suffer it to appear prima facie either in their writings or conversation: however much & however personally they or their opinions have been opposed – What now? Observe, watch those men – their habits of feeling & thinking are made up of *contempt*, which is the concentrated Vinegar of Egotism, it is Laetitia mixta cum odio/. A notion of the weakness of another conjoined with a notion of our own comparative strength, tho' that weakness is still strong enough to be *troublesome* to us (tho' not formidable) – *Die Bette thut.*

4   Philosophy and Gossip

In 1802, feeling spent, and in need of a tonic to combat the aftertaste of his own creative effervescence, Coleridge began to thirst for a lighter tone of writing. The true force of the visionary hammer-blows, that he had dreamt into literary existence while under the influence of 'the muse', had shaken him. To feel the strength of his own ideas inside him, that were not meeting with anything like reciprocation in his great friend and collaborator, Wordsworth, was hard. But Wordsworth remained unruffled by the power of *The Rime*. And, as editor of subsequent editions of *Lyrical Ballads*, he let readers know that they (discerning folk that they were) ought not to have been impressed by *The Rime*.

At the risk of losing the reader's attention, here is Wordsworth's 'Note To The Ancient Mariner', in the 1800 edition of *Lyrical Ballads*. It is as boring as a list of arbitrarily 'observed' points on a driving-test examiner's record of a borderline candidate. I only hope that the earlier analysis of *The Rime* has contextualised any Wordsworthian 'praise' of the poem as the faint, damning stuff that it is. It stands out as implacable a disavowal of Romantic sensibilities as was ever written – by the foremost of the English Romantic poets! This sort of writing should not, in this day and age, be allowed to parade before the reader without some form of counter-protest being registered. Hence, particularly offensive remarks have been under-lined, and my exclamations of indignation are within square brackets:

> I cannot refuse myself the gratification of informing such Readers as may have been pleased with this Poem, or with any part of it, that they owe their pleasure in some sort to me; as the Author was himself very desirous that it should be suppressed. This wish had arisen from a consciousness of the defects of the Poem, and from a knowledge that many persons had been much displeased with it. The Poem of my Friend has indeed great defects; first that the principal person has no distinct character, either in his profession of Mariner, or a human being who having been long under the control of supernatural impressions might be supposed himself to partake

of something supernatural: secondly, that <u>he does not act, but is continually acted upon</u> [Has this critic forgotten his *Hamlet*?]: thirdly, that the events having no necessary connection do not produce each other; and lastly, that <u>the imagery is somewhat too laboriously accumulated</u> [Rich, coming from the author of 'The Thorn']. Yet the Poem contains many delicate touches of passion, and indeed the passion is every where true to nature; a great number of the stanzas present beautiful images, and are expressed with unusual felicity of language; and <u>the versification, though the metre is itself unfit for long poems, is harmonious and artfully varied</u>, exhibiting the utmost powers of that metre, and every variety of which is capable. It therefore appeared to me that <u>these several merits (the first of which, namely that of the passion, is of the highest kind,) gave the Poem a value which is not often posessed by better Poems</u>. On this account I requested of my Friend [with 'Friend's like Wordsworth, did Coleridge need enemies?] to permit me to republish it.

Coleridge's admiration of, and subservience to, Wordsworth was – as the latter's biographer, Kenneth R. Johnson, has pointed out – practically sadomasochistic. The importance of this should not be underestimated. The fact is that the mighty, poetic *content,* in a poem like *The Rime,* elicited merely feather-light acclaim from Wordsworth. Yet Coleridge would, automatically, doubt his own (normally extremely acute) ability to assess his own literary validity.

With the understated tact of a well-meaning gentleman, Wordsworth allowed Coleridge to feel as though the latter were making a fool of himself each time he became intoxicated with the muse. Wordsworth, on the other hand, could *hold* his muse. *He* would never go over the top. He therefore set himself up as the sober apologist for any of Coleridge's giddiness in *Lyrical Ballads.* Wordsworth was simultaneously stage-hogging, and string-pulling, covertly activated, and sustained, by the involuntary impulses of self-interest. He was, in the manner of a gifted, ambitious politician, a meltingly sophisticated contriver of schemes. He could evoke an aura, or a texture, of damning implications around Coleridge, and seem not to participate in, let alone orchestrate, the artistry. He also had what is essential to the mandate-seeking politician, as he set about ingratiating himself into the favourable collective consciousness, with broad brush stroke after broad brush stroke: *stamina of mendacity.*

Neither 'Kubla Khan' nor 'Christabel' got published when Wordsworth was on the scene. And even *The Rime*, having been the poem that opened the first (1798) edition of *Lyrical Ballads*, was buried in the middle of the next edition. But, rather than dwelling for too long on the idea that Wordsworth was a sort of Herod of poetry, cruelly ordering the systematic termination of newborn, otherworldly Coleridge poems, one ought to focus on the rest of his literary progeny. Coleridge had another strain of creativity to exploit. He is far from the crestfallen, disenfranchised creature that his letter to Godwin (1801), on one level, claims he is:

> You would not know me – ! all sounds of similitude keep at such a distance from each other in my mind, that I have *forgotten* how to make a rhyme – I look at the Mountains (that visible God Almighty that looks in at all my windows) I look at the Mountains only for the Curves of their outlines; the Stars, as I behold them, form themselves into Triangles – and my hands are scarred with scratches from a Cat, whose back I was rubbing in the Dark in order to see whether the sparks were refrangible by a Prism. The Poet is dead in me – my imagination (or rather the Somewhat that had been imaginative) lies, like a Cold Snuff on the circular Rim of a Brass Candle-stick, without even a stink of Tallow to remind you that it was once cloathed and mitred with Flame. That is past by! – I was once a Volume of Gold Leaf, rising & riding on every breath of Fancy – but I have beaten myself back into weight and density, & now I sink in quicksilver, yea, remain squat on the earth amid the hurricane, that makes Oaks and Straws join in one Dance, fifty yards high in the Element.

Ebulliently articulated utterances like this do not suggest the groans of defeat. It is better to reign in prose than serve in poetry. This is philosophy-orientated talk, at once witty and weighty. It is utterly unique. "The Poet is dead in me", says Coleridge, but there is a conscious glow from his happily pregnant phrases. He found that he could sustain long flows of words and sentences high in inspiration. Here is an extract from a letter (1802) to the poet, dramatist, and translator, William Sotheby:

> It is easy to cloathe Imaginary Beings with our own Thoughts
> & Feelings; but to send ourselves out of ourselves, to *think*
> ourselves in to the Thoughts and Feelings of Beings in
> circumstances wholly & strangely different from our own/
> hoc labor, hoc opus/and who has atchieved it? Perhaps only
> Shakespere. Metaphysics is a word, that you, my dear Sir!
> are no great Friend to/but yet you will agree, that a great Poet
> must be, implicitè if not explicitè, a profound Metaphysician.
> He may not have it in logical coherence, in his Brain &
> Tongue; but he must have it by *Tact*/for all sounds, & all
> forms of human nature he must have the *ear* of a wild Arab
> listening in the silent Desart, the eye of a North American
> Indian tracing the footsteps of an Enemy upon the Leaves
> that strew the Forest – ; the *Touch* of a Blind Man fecling the
> face of a darling Child – /and do not think me a Bigot if I say,
> that I have read no French or German Writer, who appcars to
> me to have had a *heart* sufficiently pure & simple to be capable
> of this or anything like it ...

In defining what a metaphysician is, Coleridge is defining himself.
And in saying that the continental writers do not possess these criteria,
Coleridge is getting to grips with his own uniqueness in the lettered,
European scheme of things. It would ultimately embolden him to
write his prose masterpiece: *Biographia Literaria* (1817).

Nietzsche, in 1888, would complain aphoristically, and icono-
clastically, about 'What the Germans Lack', in *Twilight of the Idols*.
The Teutonic ancestry, out of which Nietzsche emerged (in spite of
himself), has imprinted its grain, similar to that which was once so
quickly acquired, in Göttingen, by Coleridge. There is little in this
Nietzsche passage that has not already been said, many decades ago,
by Coleridge:

> Learning to *think*: our schools no longer have any idea what
> this means. Even in our universities, even among students of
> philosophy themselves, the theory, the practice, the *vocation*
> of logic is beginning to die out. Read German books: no longer
> the remotest recollection that a technique, a plan of instruction,
> a will to mastery is required for thinking – that thinking has
> to be learned in the way dancing has to be learned, *as* a form

of dancing... Who among Germans still knows from experience that subtle thrill which the possession of intellectual *light feet* communicates to all the muscles! – A stiffly awkward air in intellectual matters, a clumsy hand in grasping – this is in so great a degree German that foreigners take it for the German nature in general. The German has no *fingers* for nuances ...

By 1802, the visionary, Coleridge, had been, poetically, well and truly seen off by Wordsworth. It is, clearly, the Lake District standard, as opposed to the Quantock one, that flutters above the ramparts of *Lyrical Ballads*.

It would have seemed that Coleridge was effectively exiled to a much less salubrious realm. It is worth tracing his doggedly spirited ascent to another throne.

'An Ode To The Rain' (1802) has nothing more than notorious British weather as its theme. It is a relief to talk about bad weather when divorce and suicide are fighting it out for first place in one's uppermost thoughts.

> Dear rain! if I've been cold and shy,
> Take no offence! I'll tell you why.
> A dear old Friend e'en now is here,
> And with him came my sister dear;
> After long absence now first met,
> Long months by pain and grief beset –
> We three dear friends! in truth, we groan
> Impatiently to be alone.
> We three, you mark! and not one more!
> The strong wish makes my spirit sore.
> We have so much to talk about,
> So many sad things to let out;
> So many tears in our eye-corners,
> Sitting like little Jacky Horners –
> In short, as soon as it is day,
> Do go, dear Rain! do go away.

The frivolity of both tone and topic *has* been quickly acquired. His imagination had been bubbling and steaming *so* much. Now it was not. At one point, in *The Rime*, the sun had been "flecked with bars", and made to look imprisoned, and, temporarily, powerless; in 'Kubla Khan', the "symphony and song" of the Abyssinnian maid are destined to echo forever in an almost unreachable dreamscape. However, in 'An Ode To The Rain', an entire region of sensibilities, that had been geothermically active, appears to have been cooled, and silenced, by the stroke of a wand waved for the benefit of a quitter. In the absence of supernatural danger, Coleridge's interior world has suddenly become more homely. The wild, doglike impulse, to dive into the fast-flowing unknowable, appears to have been tamed.

Perhaps the exhausted, or depleted, Coleridge has temporarily retreated from the front line to re-deploy the aspects of his genius in accordance with a deeply re-meditated plan. (Are we really to believe that Coleridge has totally given up all future attempts to revive within him the "symphony and song" of the Abyssinian maid?)

If Coleridge was merely attempting to school his imagination into a talkative, inconsequential, English poeticality, he would shortly be in for another shock. In 1803, in 'The Pains of Sleep', he would be driven to evoke the opium addict's withdrawal symptoms in a truly devastating way.

The first stanza of 'The Pains of Sleep', like the first stanza of 'Kubla Khan', is really the quiet prelude to the main psychological action. Coleridge is lulling himself to sleep, hoping (in vain) that the monsters, fiendishly awaiting his return to their habitat – his unconsciousness – will have dispersed. "But", as soon as one enters the second stanza, one realises that every byway of the narrator's unconscious is chock-a-block with hateful traffic. Look at the cumulative din and glare of the second stanza. The initially tepid conversational tone is brought rapidly, and fearfully, to the boil. Within the deliberately narrow confines of the poem's metrical structure, there is an increasingly chaotic feeling as heated syllables collide with, and bounce off, one another with increasing volatility:

> But yester-night I prayed aloud
> In anguish and in agony,
> Up-starting from the fiendish crowd
> Of shapes and thoughts that tortured me:
> A lurid light, a trampling throng,
> Sense of intolerable wrong,
> And whom I scorned, those only strong!

Thirst of revenge, the powerless will
Still baffled, and yet burning still!
Desire with loathing strangely mixed
On wild or hateful objects fixed.
Fantastic passions! maddening brawl!
And shame and terror over all!
Deeds to be hid which were not hid,
Which all confused I could not know
Whether I suffered, or I did:
For all seemed guilt, remorse or woe,
My own or others still the same
Life-stifling fear, soul-stifling shame.

20th century poetry enthusiasts have often eulogised the filmic quality of T.S. Eliot's earlier poetry, and how the reader is able to insert his or her own images between the lines of, say, 'The Love Song of J. Alfred Prufrock', 'Portrait of a Lady', or 'Preludes'. Yet, compare the confessional terror of Coleridge's "Deeds to be hid which were not hid" with Eliot's non-committal, purely visual offering in 'Preludes':

You lay upon your back, and waited;
You dozed, and watched the night revealing
The thousand sordid images
Of which your soul was constituted;
They flickered against the ceiling.

It was not at all in Coleridge's nature to formulate a brand of designer angst and advertise it as great poetry. He was suffering too much, not least when he wrote 'The Pains of Sleep'. He genuinely felt that God was punishing him for not having the strength to kick his opium habit. Medical professionals had yet to find out about the concept of addiction. As far as it was understood at the time, it was even fair enough to give a child with tummy ache a small dose of opium. Opium was frequently prescribed, for the gamut of common ailments, with the same irresponsibility, and unaccountability, shown by those doctors, today, who carelessly placate masses of patients with anti-depressants.

As Coleridge, and the increasingly unsympathetic Wordsworth, saw it, he just needed to give himself a good shake. In 'Resolution and Independence' (1802), Wordsworth alluded to Coleridge in this glibly chastising way:

> But how can He expect that others should
> Build for him, sow for him, and at his call
> Love him, who for himself will take no heed at all?

And Coleridge, in 'The Pains of Sleep', was taking cognisance of his nightmare predicament:

> Such punishments, I said, were due
> To natures deepliest stained with sin ...

At the time, Coleridge appeared to be engulfed in his own weakness of will. But it is only when his life is viewed as a connected whole that his character and capacities show themselves in their true light. Here, for example, is one of the many particular instances, one of the happy inspirations, which led Coleridge to choose the only true expression:

> For aye entempesting anew
> The unfathomable hell within ...

One may find an important psychological dimension in the literature of the modern western world distilled here. Saul Bellow's debut novel of the 40s, *Dangling Man*, mentions the formidable craters of the human spirit more than once. Their lineage may be traced back to Coleridge, whose work is unprecedentedly pockmarked by the impacts of real despair. Until Coleridge's death, in 1834, he would rarely be able to survey his own mentality without seeing such declivities. Coleridge begins 'The Garden of Boccaccio' (1828), by reviewing his own desolation:

> Of late, in one of those most weary hours,
> When life seems emptied of all genial powers,
> A dreary mood, which he who ne'er has known
> May bless his happy lot, I sate alone;
> And, from the numbing spell to win relief,
> Call'd on the Past for thought of glee or grief.
> In vain! bereft alike of grief and glee,
> I sate and cow'r'd o'er my own vacancy!

This image *is* quintessential Coleridge/Romanticism.

> And as I watch'd the dull continuous ache,
> Which, all else slumb'ring, seem'd alone to wake ...

And the following paradox, from 'The Pains of Sleep', could be all the psychological conflict, concentrated, and deftly scooped from the bottom of Dostoyevski's *Crime and Punishment* (1866):

> The horror of their deeds to view,
> To know and loathe, yet wish and do!

Coleridge is the prototype of the modern, alienated man. Enervation leaks, as it were, from his pinpricked solipsism:

> Partly from ill-health, & partly from an unhealthy & reverie-like vividness of *Thoughts*, & (pardon the pedantry of the phrase) a diminished Impressibility from *Things*, my ideas, wishes, & feelings are to a diseased degree disconnected from *motion* and *action*. In plain and natural English, I am a dreaming & therefore an indolent man.

But he celebrates his own ability to populate the desolation of the world with his animating (albeit opium-aided) thoughts:

> Laudanum gave me repose, not sleep: but YOU [Coleridge is writing, here, to his brother, George Coleridge, in 1798], I believe, know how divine that repose is – what a spot of inchantment, a green spot of fountains, & flowers & trees, in the very heart of a waste of Sands!

He is, in a way, like Duc Jean des Esseintes, J.K. Huysmans's hermit-like protagonist in *A Rebours* (1884). Des Esseintes, estranged from society, enjoyed "false, fictitious pleasures ... for instance, a man can undertake long voyages of exploration sitting in his armchair by the fireside, helping out, if needful, his recalcitrant or sluggish imagination by the perusal of some work descriptive of travels in distant lands ...". (Remember that Coleridge fell into his fructifying opium sleep while reading Purchas's *Pilgrimage*, and it would be truer to say that 'Kubla Khan' found its way through him, rather than that he created 'Kubla Khan'.)

Or, Coleridge is like Samuel Cramer, in Baudelaire's novella, *La Fanfarlo* (1847):

> the man of beautiful works which had been bungled; a sickly and fantastic creature whose poetry gleams far more in his person than in his works, and who, towards one o'clock in the morning, between the dazzling glow of his earth-coal fire and the ticking of a clock, has always seemed to me to be the god of impotence – a modern and hermaphrodite god – an impotence so colossal and enormous that it has become epic!

Baudelaire was a highly perceptive critic of, amongst many things, English Romantic literature. He had internalised the contradictions that made the creative drive in a Coleridge, or a Cramer, fitful. In *La Fanfarlo*, he simultaneously celebrates, and examines quizzically, the Romantic temperament. The fact that his protagonist is called Samuel may or may not be a coincidence:

> How can I make you fully acquainted with, how can I let you see clearly into, this dark nature, streaked with brilliant flashes of lightning – simultaneously lazy and enterprising – fertile in ambitious plans and laughable failures – a mind in which paradox often assumed the proportions of naivety, and whose imagination was as vast as his solitude and laziness were absolute?

After all, Coleridge's sonnet, 'Work Without Hope' (1825), is about inertia. Any student who has ever been overwhelmed by that strange sense of neurotic paralysis prior to examination time – when most other students appear motivated, industrious, focused, and callous – will recognise the subtly evoked, vaguely panicky stasis:

> All Nature seems at work. Slugs leave their lair –
> The bees are stirring – birds are on the wing –
> And Winter slumbering in the open air,
> Wears on his smiling face a dream of Spring!
> And I the while, the sole unbusy thing,
> Nor honey make, nor pair, nor build, nor sing.
>   Yet well I ken the banks where amaranths blow,
> Have traced the fount whence streams of nectar flow.
> Bloom, O ye amaranths! bloom for whom ye may,

For me ye bloom not! Glide, rich, streams, away!
With lips unbrightened, wreathless brow, I stroll:
And would you learn the spells that drowse my soul?
Work without Hope draws nectar in a sieve,
And Hope without an object cannot live.

At university, Coleridge had usually preferred to read stacks and
stacks of books that were *not* on the syllabus. He was, therefore,
never necessarily likely to become a first-class shoveller of exam-
iners' fodder. (He left Cambridge in December 1794, without taking
his degree.) Genius is a quantum leap away from merely first-class,
and Coleridge had already, in 1800, written, without admiration,
about the first-class nature of Robert Southey's talent:

> At college he was a severe student ... That revelry and that
> debauchery, which are so often fatal to the powers of intellect,
> would probably have been serviceable to him; they would
> have given him a closer communion with realities ...
>   The influencer of his country and of his species was a
> young man, the creature of another's predetermination
> [Coleridge is referring to Southey's father here], sheltered
> and weather-fended from all the elements of experience; a
> young man, whose feet had never wandered; whose very eye
> had never turned to the right or to the left; whose whole track
> had been as curveless as the motion of a fascinated reptile!

In 'Work Without Hope', Coleridge, as a mature poet, is both
dismayed and fascinated by his incapacity to embrace the worldly
struggle of the moment, and 'put his back into it'. He is con-
stitutionally incapable of doing what he should be doing. This has,
by nowadays, of course, become one of the celebrated/condemned
(delete according to taste) traits of the Romantic temperament. Late
19th century French literature has since provided us with energetic
arguments for apathy. Rimbaud would say that "Action is not life
but an enervating means of corrupting our strength"; Flaubert would
say that "Activity is becoming more and more distasteful to me";
and Baudelaire would provide the modern man, of wealth and taste,
with the all-important commandment, "A dandy does nothing".
Coleridge says that his attempt to "Work without Hope draws nectar
in a sieve". Fair enough. But one could muscle in on this realm of

exculpatory metaphors, swap the sieve for a bucket, and see that his intellectual lifeboat is sinking and he won't even bother to bail!

Henry Crabb Robinson, correspondent of *The Times*, was surprised, on first meeting him (in 1810), by Coleridge's consistent failure to be formidable in arguments:

> Though he practises all sorts of delightful tricks and shows admirable skill in riding his hobbies, he may be easily unsaddled. I was surprised to find how easy it is to obtain from him concessions which lead to gross inconsistencies.

But the fact that Robinson did "not feel in the least afraid of him" did not prevent him from feeling inferior to Coleridge. He said this in a letter to his brother, recounting that most extraordinary of experiences: a first meeting with Coleridge. This letter offers an invaluable insight into the nature of Coleridge the thinker. He is rather like a force of nature. Robinson's assertion of the fact that he "did not feel afraid" of Coleridge is, in fact, very revealing. Robinson was a remarkably intelligent war correspondent, and then became an equally remarkable lawyer. This portrayal of him standing, utterly rapt, before the vast, yet curiously benign, Coleridgean phenomenon, helps to put Coleridge into perspective:

> [Coleridge] kept me on the stretch of attention and admiration from half-past three till twelve o'clock. On politics, metaphysics and poetry, more especially on the Regency, Kant and Shakespeare, he was astonishingly eloquent.

Like Hamlet (who had "that within [him] which passeth show"), he amuses himself with the contents of his mind; in the manner of Hamlet, he manages to uphold his non-encroachment on others, while at the same time laying his ideas bare for examination by an audience/readership:

> My dear Friend
> I have often amused myself with the thought of a self-conscious Looking-glass, and the various metaphorical applications of such a fancy – and this morning it struck across the Eolian Harp of my Brain that there was something pleasing and emblematic (of what I did not distinctly make out) in two

such Looking-glasses fronting, each seeing the other in itself, and itself in the other. – Have you ever noticed the Vault or snug little Apartment which the Spider spins and weaves for itself, by spiral threads round and round, and sometimes with strait lines, so that it's Lurking-parlour or Withdrawing-room is an oblong square? This too connected itself in my mind with the melancholy truth, that as we grow older, the World (alas! how often it happens, that the less we love it, the more we care for it; the less reason we have to value it's Shews, the more anxious are we about them! – alas! how often do we become more and more loveless, as Love, which can outlive all change save a change with regard to itself, and all loss save the loss of it's *Reflex*, is more needed to sooth us & alone is able so to do!)

What was I saying? – O – I was adverting to the fact, that as we advance in years, the World, that *spidery* Witch, spins it's threads narrower and narrower, still closing in on us, till at last it shuts us up within four walls, walls of flues and films, windowless – and well if there be sky-lights, and a small opening left for the Light from above.

This is from a letter, written in 1825, to his confidante, Ann Gillman. His propensity to harmonise disparate metaphysical ideas (in this case, the idea of a spider spinning its web in the corner of a room, and that of a mirror reflecting another mirror) never left him.

Coleridge spent much of his career opening up new imaginative perspectives, but not going on the offensive with them:

I speak in figures, inward thoughts and woes
Interpreting by Shapes and outward Shews.
Call the World Spider: and at fancy's touch
Thought becomes image and I see it such.

This is from the same letter to Ann Gillman. His prose has condensed into verse as freely and naturally as clouds into rain. His articulation modulates as if in accordance with strange atmospheric conditions beyond the brink of syntax. He "see[s] it such." We are free not to. It is precisely in our freedom not to see things the way Coleridge does, that we are enchanted to follow his voice through the intriguing density of his peculiar idiom, to the rewarding bowers of his imagination.

But this remarkable letter writing was not profitable to Coleridge in the material sense. While the deep surge of the drive, from within Coleridge, to write like this was having its sway, Wordsworth was, professionally, and prolifically, snowballing *his* œuvre over such slushy topics as the introduction of Christianity into Britain, the consummation of the Papal Dominion, the reign of Charles I, and history since the Restoration. Wordsworth's *Ecclesiastical Sketches* (1822), later to be called *Ecclesiastical Sonnets*, were more likely to sustain his eminence than private letters and notebook entries. Coleridge had, by this stage, become a sage. None of the symptoms of formal poetic prominence could have added lustre to the unstoppable radicalism of his thought processes. Wordsworth had become a career-minded conservative unused to the manning of lookout posts in the Stygian gloom of genuine insight.

Of Donne's poetry, Coleridge wrote, in 1818:

> With Donne, whose muse on dromedary trots,
> Wreath iron pokers into true-love knots;
> Rhyme's sturdy cripple, fancy's maze and clue,
> Wit's forge and fire-blast, meaning's press and screw.

Coleridge's muse, by contrast, floated, knowingly borne on the breezes that one would think ought to make something so fragile eager to alight and take root. But for Coleridge to chalk parameters around his capriciously flourishing/withering muse would have been pointless. He needed to float, innocently receptive to, and grateful for, but guilty about, his consuming interior world that yielded little visible return.

The man, to whom so much subsequent European literature is deeply indebted, realised the absolute importance of shouldering, as little as possible, the sort of responsibilities that may have unbent the refined springs of his unassertive thinking. When he protracted his stay in Germany, in 1799, and his wife (who had lost a child in his absence) was posting pleading letters to him to return, he sent her this:

> If I had but two little wings
> And were a little feathery bird,

To you I'd fly, my dear!
But thoughts like these are idle things,
    And I stay here.

But in my sleep to you I fly:
    I'm always with you in my sleep!
    The world is all one's own.
But then one wakes, and where am I?
    All, all alone.

Sleep stays not, though a monarch bids:
    So I love to wake ere break of day:
    For though my sleep be gone,
Yet while 'tis dark, one shuts one's lids,
    And still dreams on.

Irresponsibility was his ticket to his greatness. His having been nice to his wife, or not, is neither here nor there.

The hard outlines of juxtapositions are rendered attractively unimposing in the context of Coleridge's vision. The following note-book entry (1816) is (a fact not lost on Richard Holmes) an aphoristic harbinger of the seminal *Biographia Literaria* (1817):

> If a man could pass through Paradise in a dream, and have a flower presented to him as a pledge that his soul had really been there, and if he found that flower in his hand when he awoke – Aye! and what then?

Conditioned as they were by the looming presence of the Protestant work ethic, Coleridge's recurrent anxieties never gave him any peace of mind. Underneath all the lazily accumulated (as many critics saw it) failures and successes, Coleridge could feel that the natural development of his imaginative torque was being hampered by the frequent, involuntary renewal of his own utility-orientated scruples. In a letter to John Thelwall (in 1797), he had fantasised about not having to do anything, in heavenly circumstances that did not induce one with tedious, earthly guilt for not having done anything:

> I adopt the Brahman Creed, & say – It is better to sit than to stand, it is better to lie than to sit, it is better to sleep than to

wake – but Death is the best of all! – I should much wish, like the Indian Vishna to float about along an infinite ocean cradled in the flower of the Lotos, & wake once in a million years for a few minutes – just to know that I was going to sleep a million years more.

Wordsworth emphasised the importance of passivity for a poet. Wordsworth's garden, at Dove Cottage, in Grasmere, was not weeded in accordance with the idealised, 18th century landscaping of Capability Brown. The motto at Dove Cottage was, 'if it wants to grow, let it'. But Wordsworth's attitude to horticultural matters did not – however subtly the implication was turned towards the reading public's gaze – inform his writings very significantly. Passivity too often produces too little between the signing of a contract and the arrival of a deadline. There is little point in allowing one's tapering imaginings, and wuthering mood swings, to be the only shapers of one's latest work. In his book, *Writing For Pleasure And Profit* (1986), Michael Legat articulates a truth that is surely tasteless to those capable of putting pen to paper *only* when their eyes are full of moon:

> Professional writers don't rely on inspiration. There may be occasional flashes of insight, sudden brilliant ideas, experiences which give a new urge to write or suggest a different and exciting approach, and writers seize on them gratefully. But that's not the way the bulk of the writing gets done.

Professional credibility is all. Rosemary Ashton is right to assume that Coleridge was the subject of a fragment written by Wordsworth in 1801:

> So intent upon baking his bread without leaven
> And of giving to earth the perfection of heaven,
> That he thinks and does nothing at all.

Hazlitt, who, elsewhere, had been known to write glowingly of Coleridge, was able to fire volleys of abuse, containing the buckshot of genuine insight, into his target's character:

The man of perhaps the greatest ability now living is the one who has not only done the least, but who is actually incapable of ever doing any thing worthy of him – unless he had a hundred hands to write with, and a hundred mouths to utter all that it hath entered into his heart to conceive, and centuries before him to embody the endless volume of his waking dreams.

Yet passivity is what Coleridge, in spite of his personal circumstances, practised as much as was possible in his part anarchic, part law-abiding, always troubled, conscience. Even when he wrote a letter to Davy (in 1800), defending himself against Godwin's charge that he was wasting his genius on Chemistry, Coleridge really only parodied an argumentative stance. He preferred, instead, to sweep the reader into the heady, Coleridgean parlour, and offer him, on the house, the deep draughts of his thoughts frothed over the top with humour:

Why, quoth I, how, Godwin! can you thus talk of a science, of which neither you nor I understand an iota? &c &c – & I defended Chemistry as knowingly at least as Godwin attacked it – affirmed that it united the opposite advantages of immaterializing the mind without destroying the definiteness of the Ideas – nay even while it gave clearness to them – And eke that being necessarily performed with the passion of Hope, it was poetical - & we both agreed (for G. as well as I thinks himself a Poet) that *the Poet* is the Greatest possible character – &c &c. Modest Creatures! – ... You, & I, & Godwin, & Shakespeare, & Milton, with what an athanasiophagous Grin we shall march together – *we poets*: Down with all the rest of the World! – By the word athanasiophagous I mean devouring Immortality by anticipation – 'Tis a sweet Word!

5   Plagiarist?

Coleridge plagiarised. There are passages copied word for word from Schelling in the *Biographia Literaria*.

Byron's unspeakable sin had been his 'Greek love'; Wordsworth's had been his quasi-sexual relationship with his sister, Dorothy; Coleridge's was plagiarism. The following 1802 notebook entry could be a cryptic crossword clue, so furtive is the reverberation in the absence of the first person singular: "A thief in the Candle, consuming in a blaz[e] the Tallow belonging to the wick out of sight – /Plagiary from past authors &c – ."

And just as the intensity of Wordsworth's relationship with Dorothy was not really dealt with until F.W. Bateson obliged with *Wordsworth, A Reinterpretation* (1954), so Coleridge's dirtiest linen was not fully exposed until *A History of Modern Criticism* (volume 2, 1955), by René Wellek; and *Coleridge, The Damaged Archangel* (1971), by Norman Fruman.

Coleridge was the kind of thief who did not need to steal. De Quincey exposed Coleridge's outright theft from Schelling, in the *Biographia Literaria*, but used this unbecoming instance of miscreant literary behaviour as the foil against which he showed the size of Coleridge's genius:

> Had, then, Coleridge any need to borrow from Schelling? Did he borrow *in forma pauperis*? Not at all: there lay the wonder. He spun daily, and at all hours, for mere amusement of his own activities, and from the loom of his own magical brain, theories more gorgeous by far, and supported by a pomp and luxury of images, such as neither Schelling – no, nor any German that ever breathed, not John Paul – could have emulated in his dreams. With the riches of El Dorado lying about him, he would condescend to filch a handful of gold from any man whose purse he fancied, and in fact reproduced in a new form, applying itself to intellectual wealth, that maniacal propensity which is sometimes well known to attack proprietors and millionaires for acts of petty larceny.

The critic, Thomas McFarland, has corroborated De Quincey's view with the appropriate modern terminology, by writing about Coleridge's 'kleptomania'.

We should, however, be eternally grateful to Coleridge for having martyred himself to the eternal charge of theft. The following, from a footnote in Richard Holmes' *Coleridge: Darker Reflections*, is uplifting because it puts Coleridge's petty crimes in the much more significant literary/philosophical context:

> Coleridge championed the new German criticism and idealist philosophy, adapted it and developed it in an English context, and successfully made it part of the Romantic movement. His intellectual heirs are De Quincey, Thomas Carlyle, J.S. Mill, and Matthew Arnold. It is impossible to imagine a modern view of literary form, creativity and the unconscious, or poetry itself, without Coleridge. Many of the specific concepts he was supposed to have plagiarized – such as the notion of 'organic form', the attack on the 'dramatic unities', the 'fusing' power of the imagination, the role of the dream and the symbol – have a long and complex intellectual history in 18th century criticism, German, French and English ... But time and time again it is Coleridge who formulates them most subtly and most memorably in his generation.
>
> Where he stole – and one repeats, he did steal – he also transformed, clarified and made resonant. He brought ideas to life in a unique way. Moreover, far more than any of his German sources, he always wrote as a poet. His exquisite sensitivity to language, his psychological acuity, his metaphors and extended images of explanation (as well as his sudden asides) have no equivalent in his German sources, not even in Schlegel. It is this aspect of his work that has proved most enduring ... To sum up: one can say that Coleridge plagiarized, but that no one plagiarized like Coleridge.

In today's cultural climate, plagiarism is indulged a little bit like alcoholism. As long as one can *handle* one's plagiarism, then one is not chastised too severely. In fact, one is applauded for being unacknowledgingly erudite. T.S. Eliot's unacknowledged debt to Walter Pater and many others simply cannot, in our fragment-dominated, channel-hopping milieu, be elucidated in any way that might knock Eliot off that 20th century perch of his.

In a way, Coleridge – the great literary ducker-and-diver whose only 'crime' was to be 'caught' – is tailormade for the current cultural climate of unaccountable allusiveness. A.S. Byatt's novel, *The Biographer's Tale* (2000), brings in from the cultural cold, once and for all, and gives flattering intellectual definition to, the modern penchant for ideas off the backs of lorries:

> Postmodernist ideas about intertextuality and quotation of quotation have complicated the simplistic ideas about plagiarism which were in force ... I myself think that these lifted sentences, in their new contexts, are almost the purest and most beautiful parts of the transmission of scholarship. I began a collection of them, intending, when my time came, to redeploy them with a difference, catching different light at a different angle. That metaphor is from mosaic-making. One of the things I learned in these works of research was that the great makers constantly raided previous works – whether in pebble, or marble, or glass, or silver and gold ...

As the Jacobean playwright, John Webster, once had his famous Duchess nobly protest, in a slightly different context, "Diamonds are of most value/They say, that have pass'd through most jewelers' hands." (*The Duchess of Malfi*, I, ii, 222-223.)

Regarding the attainment of critical 'acclaim' in literary England nowadays, one may be recognised as the curator of the tastefully displayed utterances of others, *not* the handler of stolen goods.

Coleridge recognised himself as a sort of node of intellectual orbits. But it pained him when he thought that it was too clear that the intellectual currents from another writer's work could not have reached his own unless he had *taken* them. He wanted it to appear as if they trickled imperceptibly, yet inevitably, from the German philosophical treatises, into his own writings, through the felicitous convolutions in the Zeitgeist! His hope that contemporary, and posthumous, academe would somehow share this psychosis was naïve in the extreme. No matter how wide-eyed Coleridge's protestations, the incriminating, obviously replicated, German material awaited cold examination (which was, eventually, forthcoming, courtesy of the fervent, mid-twentieth century tribunal: Fruman and Wellek).

So, in order to supplement his shabby defence against further charges of plagiarism (trembling as Coleridge was in the anguish of threatened discovery and degradation) he sometimes postured as the whimsical pilferer. Anything to dilute the charge of theft. He tried hard to develop a sense of humour about this. There could be no other reason for the title, and sub-title, of the poem that he wrote in 1823:

The Reproof and Reply

Or, The Flower-Thief's Apology, for a robbery committed in Mr and Mrs —'s garden, on Sunday morning, 25th of May, 1823, between the hours of eleven and twelve.

The surface meaning is clear. The fifty year old Coleridge has just purloined a handful of his next door neighbour's flowers. His neighbour scolds him:

'You, that knew better! In broad open day,
Steal in, steal out, and steal our flowers away?
What could possess you? Ah! sweet youth, I fear
The chap with horns and tail was at your ear!'

Or, rather, the charge is read out in the court of Coleridge's guilty mind.

It was first published in 1834, prefixed with the motto: "I expect no sense worth listening to, from the man who never does talk nonsense." By the time it reaches the page, the literary anxiety of the autumnal Coleridge has been craftily permeated with a summer haze of comedy:

Such sounds of late, accusing fancy brought
From Chisholm to the Poet's thought.
Now hear the meek Parnassian youth's reply: –
A bow – a pleading look – a downcast eye, –
And then …

The corpulent Coleridge could not, in his wildest dreams, have passed himself off as an apple-cheeked, orchard-raiding urchin.

So, what are the remaining 46 lines of the poem really about? Well, Coleridge, amid a foppish flutter of mock-epic phrases and epithets, casts himself as the young (!) poet entranced by the loveliness of the ground upon which he trespasses, "Beside the vocal

fount of Helicon!". He attempts to laugh himself off the hook with
winningly callow bombast:

> Say, can you blame? No! none that saw and heard
> Could blame a bard, that he thus inly stirr'd ...

The 'youth' has been 'bewitched' into acting in a way that, in normal
circumstances, would be theft:

> But most of *you*, soft warblings, I complain!
> 'Twas ye that from the bee-hive of my brain
> Did lure the fancies forth, a freakish rout,
> And witch'd the air with dreams turn'd inside out.

But the above possesses an intensity that itself could be vindication
enough for its author's petty thieving. Apart from the rousing
'intentional alliterativeness', learned originally from Spenser, this
conjures the sort of hard-to-paraphrase dream-scenery with which
Coleridge, at his best, had furnished the 'charmed sleep' of *The Rime*.
'The Reproof and Reply' is a hauntingly persuasive denial of first-
degree guilt, regarding plagiarism. With an off-the-wall impetuosity,
below and within his years, Coleridge argues that he was, in fact,
sleepwalking when he, for want of a more appropriate word, stole.
And, in this respect, he was at one with the universe:

> All Nature *day-dreams* in the month of May.
> And if I pluck'd 'each flower that *sweetest* blows,' –
> Who walks in sleep, needs follow must his *nose*.

Diehard keepers of the faith of flat language would, no doubt, pounce
on this overenthusiastic analogising as clear evidence of, in fact, a
plagiarist on the run from justice. But Coleridge knows that, in the
realm of imaginative writing, where the hunt for truth is given priority
over the hunt for facts, his own science of analogising is so exquisitely
refined as to leave whole works winnowed beyond opprobrium.

Coleridge heedlessly misquotes Wordsworth's 'Intimations of
Immortality' ode. Of course he could have quoted it correctly. But
he is making a point. Genius does not borrow, and doff its hat in the
direction of the lender. Genius steals and makes better.

His seriousness, and commitment, swells under the surface

humour of the poem. By the end, the momentum of Coleridge's metaphorical defence has, clearly, been designed to outstrip that of any syllogistic prosecution:

> Thus, long accustom'd on the twy-fork'd hill,
> To pluck both flower and floweret at my will;
> The garden's maze, like No-man's-land, I tread,
> Nor common law, nor statute in my head;
> For my own proper smell, sight, fancy, feeling,
> With autocratic hand at once repealing
> Five Acts of Parliament 'gainst private stealing!
> But yet from Chisholm who despairs of grace?
> There's no spring-gun or man-trap in *that* face!
> Let Moses then look black, and Aaron blue,
> That look as if they had little else to do:
> For Chisholm speaks, 'Poor youth! he's but a waif!
> The spoons all right? the hen and chickens safe?
> Well, well, he shall not forfeit our regards –
> The Eighth Commandment was not made for Bards!'

So, there he is, trying his best not to blush amidst bucolic scenes. What are we to think about him? Well, one could protest that imitation was, in the 18th century, a dignified form of 'stealing'. And Coleridge was an 18th, before he was a 19th century poet.

However, one does not need to rally round STC, attempting to protect his reputation with reminders of eighteenth century literary decorum. Given the sort of poetry already admired by this study, it is hardly surprising that the poet 'in the dock' has formulated a defence with much, much more life in it. The following are the criteria – from Coleridge's 1811-12 lectures – against which one should measure this genius for oneself:

ON READERS

READERS may be divided into four classes:
1. Sponges, who absorb all they read, and return it nearly in the same state, only a little dirtied.
2. Sand-glasses, who retain nothing, and are content to get through a book for the sake of getting through the time.
3. Strain-bags, who retain merely the dregs of what they read.

4. Mogul diamonds, equally rare and valuable, who profit
   by what they read, and enable others to profit by it also.

The efforts of lettered men are often, gleefully, derided for being divorced from all possible utility. The letters of this particular lettered man more so, in that others were known to accuse him of proffering gobbledygook. Byron's dismissal (in the Dedication to Canto I of *Don Juan*, 1819) of needlessly foggy verbosity was influential:

> Explaining metaphysics to the nation –
> I wish he would explain his Explanation.

Why bother trying to see whether or not there *is* the pressure of committed philosophy behind Coleridge's long sentences, replete with their exploratory sub-clauses? Having, and making, fun makes more immediate sense. Byron's fun, particularly, is irresistible.

It is, however, advisable to be entertained, rather than instructed, by Byron's rapier rhymes. (Byron's having referred to Plato as 'a bore', in *Don Juan*, ought not to put us off reading *Phaedo*, *Symposium*, or *The Republic*!) For all Byron's wit, and his enormous influence, there is no Byronic dimension to the evolution of metaphysical ideas in Europe. There is a copy of Kant's *Grundlegung zur Metaphysik der Sitter*, annotated by Coleridge, in which Coleridge attacks Kant's limited metaphors. Newton formulated his seminal scientific ideas in the language of Newtonian mathematics. (In a letter to Poole – 1801 – Coleridge remarked, with breathtaking intuition, on Newton's system, that "there is ground for suspicion that any system built on the passiveness of the mind must be false, as a system.") Coleridge formulated Romanticism in his own language of metaphors and allusions. The result – *Biographia Literaria* – is written in a warmly inviting style that incites the reader to think in terms both precise *and* manifold, regarding the definition of Romanticism. But what is Romanticism?

6   Romanticism Defined
Biographia Literaria

Aimed only at intellectuals qualified to appreciate the flamboyant metaphors and allusions fired from STC's scholarly hip, the *Biographia* certainly drew out the fatuity of its first reviewers. The following is from the *British Critic*'s learned lamentation: "... incidental criticisms upon Behmen, and Shilling [sic], and Fichti [sic], and Kant, and other inscrutible thinkers". The *New Monthly Review* reported that Coleridge's prose was "intermingled with such a cloudiness of metaphysical jargon in the mystical language of the Platonists and schoolmen, of Kant and Jacob Behmen." The *New Annual Register* complained of its "unintelligible ... metaphysics". There were not many literary journalists able to exercise a willing suspension of readerly laziness. And hope of any lull in their ignorance, willing or unwilling, would have been futile.

Perhaps the most stimulatingly combative review of the *Biographia* came from William Hazlitt:

> Mr Coleridge has ever since, from the combined forces of poetic levity and metaphysic bathos, been trying to fly, not in the air, but underground – playing at hawk and buzzard between sense and nonsense, – floating or sinking in fine Kantean categories, in a state of suspended animation 'twixt dreaming and awake, – quitting the plain ground of 'history and particular facts' for the first butterfly theory, fancy-bred from the maggots of his brain, – going up in an air-balloon filled with fetid gas from the writings of Jacob Behmen and the mystics, and coming down in a parachute made of the soiled and fashionable leaves of the Morning Post, – promising us an account of the Intellectual System of the Universe, and putting us off with a reference to a promised dissertation on the Logos ...

So there we have it. Coleridge the obscure. Or, as Tom Paulin says, Coleridge the "flaccid, turgid balloonist whose style is not 'succinct'." Even nowadays, the thicket of critical briars that has since grown up around the *Biographia* may too easily obscure the essential messages.

Having acknowledged the existence of the *Biographia*'s encircling barrier of abrasive appraisals, it is now the business of this chapter to encourage the reader to balloon directly into some of the many chambers of its obvious magnificence. Look at the following simile, in Chapter 7 of the *Biographia*, about the mechanism of *thought*. Once you *feel* the truth of it right through you, you can grasp why the imaginative writer's work rate often seems to consist of untidily intermingled fits of laziness and industriousness:

> Most of my readers [will have perceived] a small water-insect on the surface of rivulets ... and will have noticed, how the little animal *wins* its way up against the stream, by alternative pulses of active and passive motion, now resisting the current, and now yielding to it in order to gather strength and a momentary *fulcrum* for a further propulsion. This is no unapt emblem of the mind's self-experience in the act of thinking. There are evidently two powers at work, which relatively to each other are active and passive; and this is not possible without an intermediate faculty, which is at once both active and passive. (In philosophical language, we must denominate this intermediate faculty in all its degrees and determinations, the *IMAGINATION* ...

In the same way that the yoga expert is able to *feel* physically aware of his pancreas inside him as distinct from his stomach, so Coleridge is able to *feel* the viscera of his creative self:

> The *Imagination* then I consider either as primary, or secondary. The primary imagination I hold to be the living power and prime agent of all human perception, and as a repetition in the finite mind of the eternal act of creation in the infinite I AM. The secondary I consider as an echo of the former, co-existing with the conscious will, yet still as identical with the primary in the *kind* of its agency, and differing only in *degree*, and in the *mode* of its operation. It dissolves, diffuses, dissipates, in order to re-create; or where this process is rendered impossible, yet still, at all events, it struggles to idealize and to unify. It is essentially *vital*, even as all objects (as objects) are essentially fixed and dead.
>
> *Fancy*, on the contrary, has no other counters to play with, but fixities and definites. The Fancy is indeed no other than a

mode of memory emancipated from the order of time and space; and blended with, and modified by that empirical phenomenon of the will, which we express by the word choice. But equally with the ordinary memory, it must receive all its materials ready made from the law of association.

Associationism had been incorporated into Coleridge's system of thought many years before the appearance of the *Biographia*. David Hartley (1705-57), the philosopher and physician, had developed a theory of mental activity based on sound-like vibrations. For Hartley, the existence of these vibrations explained how messages were transmitted in the nervous system. What really absorbed Coleridge was Hartley's idea (associationism) that the existence of these vibrations would also explain how disparate ideas are resonated into (imaginative) togetherness in the mind. As early as 1801, Coleridge had been observing the play of his own mind, even as it writhed in the pain of unrequited love with Asra:

> Prest to my bosom & felt there – it was quite dark. I looked intensely toward her face – & sometimes I *saw* it – so vivid was the spectrum, that it had almost all its natural sense of *distance* & *outness* – except indeed that, feeling & all, I felt her as *part* of my being – twas all spectral – But when I could not absolutely *see* her, no effort of fancy could bring out even the least resemblance of her face. – .. Lazy Bed – Green [? Marine] – the fits of L[ight] & D[ark] from the Candle going out in the Socket. – Power of association – that last Image how lovely to me now –

And look at Coleridge – still in 1801 – marvelling at the deliverances of the association of ideas. He is like some mystical instrument, strung in accordance with the inconceivable musicality of an absent maestro. Coleridge is forced to admit his ignorance of how to pluck/ bow the strings in him, for the desired imaginative counterpoint: "By thinking of different parts of her Dress I can at times recall her face – but not so vividly as when it comes of itself – & therefore I have ceased to try it."

For Hartley, and the English philosopher, John Locke (1632- 1704), a new born baby's mind was a blank slate – tabula rasa – which would, over the years, passively become chalk-marked into complex maturity by every scrape of experience. Coleridge rejected this materialistic view of the mind. His excitement at going beyond this narrow conception energises his philosophical writing in Chapters 5-13. In Chapter 9, he subtly asserts that "We learn all things indeed by *occasion* of experience; but the very facts so learnt force us inward on the antecedents, that must be pre-supposed in order to render experience itself possible." It is not the Lockean, machine-like quality of the mind at which Coleridge marvels, it is its transcendental nature. After all, how could a mere machine possess intuition?

Coleridge reinvigorates one's awareness of the probability that reason and perception are not the only means through which human beings may obtain knowledge or belief. The waters upon which serious philosophy now found itself had deepened into unfathomability. Serious poetry, too, looked very different, eerily afloat on a suddenly limitless psychological depth. 'Kubla Khan', *The Rime of the Ancient Mariner* and 'Christabel' would sit differently in the light of the *Biographia*. And any psychological content in subsequently published poetry would appear at once veiled and glorified by the oblique rays of the *Biographia*'s radiant, often mystical, theorising. Wordsworth's *The Prelude* (eventually published in its 14-book format in 1850) would thus be back-lit by Coleridge's luminary critique. The following, from the *Biographia*, exemplifies this:

> Like a green field reflected in a calm and perfectly transparent lake, the image is distinguished from the reality only by its greater softness and lustre. Like the moisture or the polish on a pebble, genius neither distorts nor false-colours its objects; but on the contrary brings out many a vein and many a tint, which escape the eye of common observation, thus raising to the rank of gems what had been often kicked away by the hurrying foot of the traveller on the dusty highroad of custom.
>
> Let me refer to the whole description of skating ... especially to the lines [Coleridge quotes from Wordsworth's *Prelude*]

> > So through the darkness and the cold we flew,
> > And not a voice was idle: with the din
> > Meanwhile the precipices rang aloud;

The leafless trees and every icy crag
Tinkled like iron; while the distant hills
Into the tumult sent an alien sound
Of melancholy, not unnoticed, while the stars
Eastward were sparkling clear, and in the west
The orange sky of evening died away.

Importantly, Coleridge's philosophical explication of Wordsworth's poetry is very far from a demystification of it. Nothing is unflatteringly unpacked into (to use Wordsworth's words) "the light of common day"; and nothing is critically unpicked. But there is method in Coleridge's Romanticism. He accepts the fact that Wordsworth's insights are very special, but Coleridge does not attempt to explain how Wordsworth has set about reeling these insights up out of the depths, into common view:

> No frequency of perusal can deprive them of their freshness.
> For though they are brought into the full daylight of every
> reader's comprehension, yet they are drawn up from depths
> which few in any age are privileged to visit, into which few
> in any age have courage or inclination to descend.

Still, today, no scientific instrument exists to sound the sea of mystery in which the greatest poets have productively fished. The neuroscientist and director of the Royal Institution, Professor Susan Greenfield, admits that, while the electroencephalograph may be able to record the brain's electrical activity, there is much work to be done before we know, empirically, whether or not one's will is free. Enlightenment or no Enlightenment, Darwinism or not, the *Biographia* has retained and renewed its persuasive touch of enchantment.

Coleridge begins Chapter 10 by brandishing a neologism, "Esemplastic". Having grabbed the reader's attention anew with this provocative one word sentence, he explains that he constructed it himself. It concerns the synthesising power of the imagination: "i.e. to shape into one; because, having to convey a new sense, I thought that a new term would both aid the recollection of my meaning, and prevent its being confounded with the usual import of the word, imagination."

So, a baby's growth into adulthood is not the result of its mind's passive accumulation of experiences. Yes, 'Fancy' is responsible for the 'mechanical' function that occurs in the mind when ideas, or images, are thoughtlessly hummed together on a contingent network of sound-like vibrations. But 'Imagination' inhabits the whole with the full, autocratic refulgence of a mystical power worthy of worship.

All humans possess primary imagination. Primary imagination is a repeater, a copier. It cannot produce original works. The secondary imagination takes that which has been perceived and melts it down with thoroughgoing poetic integrity. Then it re-blends all the utterly separated elements into a genuine imitation of that which has been perceived, *not* a copy. It is the importance of this – regarding Coleridge's understanding of creativity – which the modern reader must recognise as pivotal. Coleridge's treatise is really his apology for perceived plagiarism – i.e. this is how creativity works – pitched at the highest intellectual level.

Chapters 1-4 are mainly autobiographical in content. So, behind this off and on narrative mist, of information and misinformation, Coleridge will, later, be able to smuggle in German philosophers' ideas. Schelling's (1775-1854) expansion of Fichte's idea – that there is one reality, the infinite and absolute Ego, and that nature is an absolute being working towards self-consciousness – was definitely a major source of contraband intellectualism in which the author of the *Biographia* dealt. Anti-Coleridge lobbyists could say, with justice, that Coleridge's secondary imagination's meltdown department failed to process much of the raw German material fed covertly into it.

But the fact that there have been major reservations about the validity of the *Biographia* as a classic work of literature makes it all the more remarkable that it is. Marilyn Butler has defined precisely what it is that has propelled the book's reputation beyond the atmosphere of reproach:

> What does emerge ... most brilliantly with and through Coleridge, is a new recognition of the distinctiveness of the poet as a type. It was Coleridge who in the second decade of the century, that Restoration era when so many German and French painters were creating soulful, alienated portraits of themselves and one another, produced his English writerly equivalent, the *Biographia Literaria*.

In Chapter 1, the chatty, artless elegance of the prose style is hard to resist. In the following instance, Coleridge explains past decisions to leave certain awkward parts of his earlier poetry unaltered, in the face of criticism that he acknowledges to have been more nurturing than nasty:

> In the after editions I pruned the double epithets with no sparing hand, and used my best efforts to tame the swell and glitter both of thought and diction; though, in truth, these parasite plants of youthful poetry had insinuated themselves into my longer poems with such intricacy of union, that I was often obliged to omit disentangling the weed, from the fear of snapping the flower.

Coleridge's overestimation of William Bowles' sonnets is interesting, not because of what it has to say about Bowles, but because of what it has to say about Coleridge's intellectual/imaginative development. Coleridge was 17 when he first came across the poetry of Bowles, a talented, older contemporary. Coleridge articulates the warmth that the reader can feel for the writer:

> The great works of past ages seem to a young man things of another race, in respect to which his faculties must remain passive and submiss, even as to the stars and mountains. But the writings of a contemporary, perhaps not many years older than himself, surrounded by the same circumstances, and disciplined by the same manners, possess a reality for him, and inspire an actual friendship as of a man for a man. His very admiration is the wind which fans and feeds his hope. The poems themselves assume the properties of flesh and blood.

In his famous first novel, *The Catcher in the Rye* (1951), J.D. Salinger portrays the developing intellect of the adolescent, Holden Caulfield. Caulfield ingenuously speaks his mind about his reading experiences:

> I read a lot of classical books, like *The Return of the Native* and all, and I like them, and I read a lot of war books and mysteries and all, but they don't knock me out too much, What really knocks me out is a book that, when you're all done reading it, you wish the author that wrote it was a terrific

friend of yours and you could call him up on the phone whenever you felt like it.

Caulfield's is, of course, a different brand of artless candour from that of Coleridge. But it is artless candour nonetheless, whose lineage may be traced back to the *Biographia*.

Coleridge's remarks on critics, in Chapter 3, convey the anger of a lettered man whose poet friends (Southey and Wordsworth) have been pilloried by anonymous reviewers. This culminates in the couple of sentences that ought to be compulsory reading for celebrity critics:

> He who tells me that there are *defects* in a new work, tells me nothing which I should not have taken for granted without his information. But he who points out and elucidates the *beauties* of an original work, docs indeed give me interesting information, such as experience would not have authorized me in anticipating ...

It was in Chapter 4 that Coleridge started to advertise Wordsworth's genius:

> It was the union of deep feeling with profound thought; the fine balance of truth in observing, with the imaginative faculty in modifying, the objects observed; and, above all, the original gift of spreading the tone, the *atmosphere*, and with it the depth and height of the ideal world, around forms, incidents, and situations of which, for the common view, custom had bedimmed all the lustre, had dried up the sparkle and the dew-drops ... To carry on the feelings of childhood into the powers of manhood; to combine the child's sense of wonder and novelty with the appearances which every day for perhaps forty years had rendered familiar ... this is the character and privilege of genius ...

If Wordsworth is monumental on the English cultural landscape, then Coleridge's *Biographia* was certainly instrumental in hoisting the figure up into contemporary, and posthumous, view. In the later chapters, Coleridge would instruct the reading nation how to appreciate Wordsworth's poetry. But look at what he says about Wordsworth's 'Intimations' ode:

> ... the ode was intended for such readers only as had been accustomed to watch the flux and reflux of their inmost nature, to venture at times into the twilight realms of consciousness, and to feel a deep interest in modes of inmost being, to which they knew that the attributes of time and space are inapplicable and alien, but which yet cannot be conveyed, save in symbols of time and space.

Has not Coleridge, himself, watched "the flux and reflux of [his own] inmost nature"? Has not Coleridge ventured "into the twilight realms of consciousness," and felt "a deep interest in modes of inmost being, to which [he] knew that the attributes of time and space are inapplicable and alien"? Why is Coleridge apportioning another writer with the credit that is really due to Coleridge above all others?

Look at the following, from a letter to Josiah Wade, written in 1814, just before Coleridge began to write the *Biographia*. Pay particular attention to the second sentence (italics added) in the second paragraph:

> Dear Sir,
>
> For I am unworthy to call any good man friend – much less you, whose hospitality and love I have abused; accept, however, my intreaties for your forgiveness, and for your prayers.
>
> Conceive a poor miserable wretch, who for many years has been attempting to beat off pain, by a constant recurrence to the vice that reproduces it. *Conceive a spirit in hell, employed in tracing out for others the road to that heaven, from which his crimes exclude him!* In short, conceive whatever is most wretched, helpless, and hopeless, and you will form as tolerable a notion of my state, as it is possible for a good man to have.
>
> I used to think the text in St James that 'he who offended in one point, offends in all,' very harsh; but I now feel the awful, the tremendous truth of it. In the one crime of OPIUM, what crime have I not made myself guilty of! – Ingratitude to my Maker! and to my benefactors – injustice! *and unnatural cruelty to my poor children*! – self-contempt for my repeated promise – breach, nay, too often, actual falsehood!
>
> After my death, I earnestly entreat, that a full and unqualified narration of my wretchedness, and of its guilty

cause, may be made public, that at least some little good may be effected by the direful example!

May God Almighty bless you, and have mercy on your still affectionate, and in his heart, grateful –

S.T. Coleridge

This comes from a man about to eulogise lesser talents in the stagy, floodlit glare of his own penitence.

In the *Biographia*, Coleridge's generosity may be explained by quite a straightforward psychological fact. It is, in one of its manifestations, the guilt of the partially reformed drug-addict. For Coleridge to be able to write the *Biographia*, he really had to exercise enormous willpower, working regularly every day, at Highgate, under the stern but sympathetic regime of the physician, James Gillman. Gillman regulated Coleridge's supply of opium in an effort to rehabilitate him as a writer. Having for too many years been awash on a sea of desultory reflections, Coleridge was determined that, with Gillman's sound medical help, he would produce something worthy of his genius. The *Biographia* was originally intended to have been a much shorter Preface to a collection of poems, to rival Wordsworth's Preface and *his* new collection. However, once Coleridge became fully embroiled in the task of siphoning enough of his inner maelstrom onto publishable pages, competing with his old collaborator became irrelevant.

On the new moral scaffolding of regular work habits, Coleridge built the crooked timber of personal aesthetic opinions up around his past. The *Biographia* is Coleridge's deeply apologetic gift to the milieu, and to posterity, for having treated everybody so very badly: his children, family, friends, and his readership.

One could argue that Coleridge's secondary imagination "dissolves, diffuses and dissipates" all the detail of his neglectful behaviour into one big, throbbing, amorphous impulse of intense humility – the spirit of shame. It becomes the spirit most responsible for securing possession of readers whose minds involuntarily dilate in Romantic gloom. It inhabits the interior of the *Biographia* like a troubled, maundering soul that cannot quite refine itself into consistent invisibility. It haunts certain corridors, and passageways, of the prose's rickety structure. Here, it clanks along, brazenly offering German philosophers' ideas. There, it slips through what looks like a conversational brick wall to the reader (but is a communicating door to the ghost) with diffident, and even obsequious gestures. It may even whisper its weaknesses, and failures, as seductive confidences:

> Prudence itself would command us to *show*, even if defect or diversion of natural sensibility had prevented us from *feeling*, a due interest and qualified anxiety for the offspring and representatives of our nobler being. I know it, alas! by woeful experience! I have laid too many eggs in the hot sands of this wilderness, the world, with ostrich carelessness and ostrich oblivion. The greater part, indeed, have been trod under foot, and are forgotten; but yet no small number have crept forth into life, some to furnish feathers for the caps of others, and still more to plume the shafts in the quivers of my enemies, of them that unprovoked have lain in wait against my soul.

It is very common for young people to breathe the vivifying air of failure, with a view to quietly developing the gorgeous wings with which they intend, sooner or later, to fly elsewhere. But it is not where you fly. It is what you take with you, inside. Coleridge's awareness of this, coupled, as it is, with a strident belief in the transcendental nature of this inner power, is way, way ahead of its time:

> ... the wings of the air-sylph are forming within the skin of the caterpillar; those only, who feel in their own spirits the same instinct which impels the chrysalis of the horned fly to leave room in its involucrum for antennae yet to come. They know and feel that the *potential* works *in* them, even as the actual works on them! In short, all the organs of sense are framed for a corresponding world of sense, and we have it. All the organs of spirit are framed for a corresponding world of spirit: though the latter organs are not developed in all alike. But they exist in all, and their first appearance discloses itself in the *moral* being. How else could it be, that even worldlings, not wholly debased, will contemplate the man of simple and disinterested goodness with contradictory feelings of pity and respect? 'Poor man! he is not for this world.' Oh! herein they utter a prophecy of universal fulfilment; for a man must either rise or sink ...

7   Coleridge as Critic

Coleridge, an immensely original man, stole others' ideas and lied about it. He regularly misinformed his closest friends about his sterling, professional writer's habits. He would lie about how far on he was with a piece of work expected by impatient publishers. He often got into depressingly slovenly ruts, lying in bed until well into the afternoon. As in the cases of his friendships with Southey and Wordsworth, he could enchant, and influence, clever men, but this would often be followed by his driving them away with his clinging, needy temperament.

Yet, in the quiet of his own company, he existed, intellectually, on a different wavelength. To be properly picked up – *received* – it was a wavelength possessed by late twentieth/early twenty-first century readers. This chapter concerns the frequency at which Coleridge transmitted his profundity.

On first meeting STC, John Keats' highly unusual sensitivity apprehended the seemingly jumbled data of Coleridge's thinking:

> I walked with him at his alderman-after-dinner pace for near two miles I suppose. In these two miles he broached a thousand things. – let me see if I can give you a list. – Nightingales, Poetry – on Poetical sensation – Metaphysics – Different genera and species of Dreams – Nightmare – a dream accompanied by a sense of Touch – single and double Touch – A dream related – First and Second Consciousness – the difference explained between Will and Volition – so many metaphysicians from a want of smoking the second Consciousness – Monsters – the Kraken – Mermaids – Southey believes in them – Southey's belief too much diluted – A Ghost Story – Good morning. – I heard his voice as he came towards me – I heard it as he moved away – I heard it all the interval – if it may be called so.

It took Keats to articulate the sense of timeless, exotic riches borne on the vivifying thrum of Coleridge's voice.

The Zeitgeist breathed by Southey, Wordsworth, Hazlitt, and others, positively *teemed* with Coleridgean emissions spiralling in the intellectual/imaginative magnetic field. But Coleridge's contemporaries, whether or not they were leagued against him in a conspiracy of faint praise, failed to broadcast the truth of his greatly superior significance. It is *we* in the 21st century that may be more profitably haunted by the charged particles and magnetic fields of the cold, thin gas between the flickering, distant Coleridge and us. His contemporaries could be forgiven for often feeling nonplussed by the white noise of his talk, talk, talk. De Quincey writes reasonably about this:

> This eternal stream of talk which never for one instant intermitted, and allowed no momentary opportunity of reaction to the persecuted and bated auditor, was absolute ruin to the interests of the talker himself. Always passive – always acted upon, never allowed to react, into what state did the poor afflicted listener – he that played the *role* of listener – collapse? He returned home in the exhausted condition of one that has been drawn up just before death from the bottom of a well occupied by foul gasses; and, of course, hours before he had reached that perilous point of depression, he had lost all power of distinguishing, understanding, or connecting.

The Scottish essayist and historian, Thomas Carlyle, who received the entirety of Goethe's utterances as a divine opus, was decidedly less impressed by STC's sonic litter: "I have heard [him] talk, with eager musical energy, two stricken hours, his face radiant and moist, and communicate no meaning whatsoever to any individual of his hearers."

But a couple of centuries' fluctuating critical reception has resolved Coleridgeanism into a timeless susurrus of sagacity. The following notebook entry has force enough to reach us underneath the noise of modern life:

> The most melancholy time after the death of a Friend, or Child is when you first awake after your first Sleep/when the dizziness, heat & drunkenness of Grief is gone/ and the pang of hollowness is first felt.

Coleridge's interest is greatly aroused by the feelings that momentarily rear above the bland surface of our lives:

Few moments in life so interesting as those of an affectionate reception from those who have heard of you yet are strangers to your person.

Coleridge was the first writer to consistently articulate the psychological alloy of reality and unreality that constitutes most modern mentalities. The following (1803) notebook entry could be that of any disorientated observer of the position of an electron inside an atom:

Mix up Truth & Imagination, so that the Imag. May spread its own indefiniteness over that which really happened, & Reality its sense of substance & distinctness to Imagination/ For the Soother of Absence –

Mining the seam between consciousness and unconsciousness, Coleridge was the first thinker to attempt something approaching the systematic retrieval of precious insights crystallised, as it were, in the human soul. The following is an 1803 notebook entry:

Frid. Morn. 5 o'clock – Dosing, dreamt of Hartley as at his Christening – how as he was asked who redeemed him, & was to say, God the Son/ he went on, humming and hawing, in one hum & haw, like a boy who knows a thing & will not make the effort to recollect it – so as to irritate me greatly. Awakening (gradually [I found] I was able completely to detect, that) it was the Ticking of my Watch which lay in the Pen Place in my Desk on the round Table close by my Ear, & which in the diseased State of my Nerves had *fretted* on my Ears – I caught the fact while Hartley's Face & moving Lips were yet before my Eyes, & his Hum & Ha, & the Ticking of the Watch were each the other, as often happens in the passing off of Sleep – that curious modification of Ideas by each other … I arose instantly, & wrote it down – it is now 10 minutes past 5.

In this context, initially, opium was his 'Davy lamp', enabling him to work for prolonged periods in the dark depths of his own psyche. De Quincey's celebrated assertion of 'The Pleasures of Opium' applies, emphatically, here:

> ... opium ...(if taken in a proper manner), introduces amongst [the mental faculties] the most exquisite order, legislation, and harmony... opium sustains and reinforces [one's self-possession] ... opium ... communicates serenity and equipoise to all the faculties, active or passive; and, with respect to the temper and moral feelings in general, it gives simply that sort of vital warmth which is approved by the judgment, and which would probably always accompany a bodily constitution of primeval or antediluvian health.

Coleridge was the first real modern critic of Shakespeare – who understood what pleasure, but what anguish, it is to be alive. It is not very surprising that the author of the 'Dejection' ode would be responsible for revolutionising the way the character of Hamlet was perceived. Until Coleridge's Shakespeare lectures, *Hamlet* was seen as an "inexplicable ... misgrowth ... of the capricious and irregular genius of Shakespeare." Coleridge would reveal Shakespeare's almost miraculously consistent psychological validity. There is much edification for the reader of these radical lectures. They have stood the test of time. One genius has unlocked the treasure-chest of another genius' glittering art. There is something of the sense of Coleridge's face reflecting the sudden blaze of hidden Shakespearean wealth that greets, dazzlingly, the first successful picker of the Bard's lock. It took one to know one. Look at this interpretation of Hamlet's erratic, and profitless, behaviour:

> ... Hamlet's mind ... unseated from its healthy relations, is constantly occupied with the world within, and abstracted from the world without, – giving substance to shadows, and throwing a mist over all common-place actualities. It is the nature of thought to be indefinite; – definiteness belongs to external imagery alone. Hence it is that a sense of sublimity arises, not from the sight of an outward object, but from the beholder's reflection upon it; – not from the sensuous impression, but from the imaginative reflex.

Most mentalities are made of the 'normal' amalgam of the subjective and the objective. Coleridge is receptive to Shakespeare's study of an improperly amalgamated mentality. He is receptive because he recognises the symptoms in himself (such as "that craving after the indefinite" which Hazlitt relished ridiculing).

When Coleridge lectures on Hamlet, he is really lecturing on himself: "He mistakes the seeing his chains for the breaking them, delays action till action is of no use". And every sentence of Coleridge's literary criticism has authority about it – the authority of a man who has read, and lived:

> These complex causes will naturally have produced in Hamlet the disposition to escape from his own feelings of the overwhelming and supernatural by a wild transition to the ludicrous, – a sort of cunning bravado, bordering on the flights of delirium. For you may, perhaps, observe that Hamlet's wildness is but half false; he plays that subtle trick of pretending to act only when he is very near really being what he acts.

In his lecture on *Romeo and Juliet*, Coleridge anatomises love-orientated humankind:

> Considering myself and my fellow-men as a sort of link between heaven and earth, being composed of body and soul, with power to reason and to will, and with that perpetual aspiration which tells us that this is ours for a while, but it is not ourselves; considering man, I say, in this two-fold character, yet united in one person, I conceive that there can be no correct definition of love which does not correspond with our being, and with that subordination of one part to another which constitutes our perfection. I would say therefore that –
>
> 'Love is a desire of the whole being to be united to some thing, or some being, felt necessary to its completeness, by the most perfect means that nature permits, and reason dictates.'

When Coleridge writes of Romeo's loves, he is surely informed by his own experiences with Sarah Fricker, and then Asra:

> Shakespeare has described this passion in various states and stages beginning, as was most natural, with love in the young. Does he open his play by making Romeo and Juliet in love at first sight – at the first glimpse, as any ordinary thinker would

do? Certainly not: he knew what he was about: he was to develop the whole passion, and he commences with the first elements – that sense of imperfection, that yearning to combine itself with something lovely. Romeo became enamoured of the idea he had formed in his own mind, and then, as it were, christened the first real being of the contrary sex as endowed with the perfections he desired. He appears to be in love with Rosaline; but, in truth, he is in love only with his own idea. He felt that necessity of being beloved which no noble mind can be without. Then our poet, our poet who so well knew human nature, introduces Romeo to Juliet, and makes it not only a violent, but a permanent love – a point for which Shakespeare has been ridiculed by the ignorant and unthinking. Romeo is first represented in a state most susceptible of love, and then, seeing Juliet, he took and retained the infection.

Coleridge's estimation of Shakespeare's genius is boldly adulatory for its time:

Shakespeare knew the human mind, and its most minute and intimate workings, and he never introduces a word, or a thought, in vain or out of place: if we do not understand him, it is our own fault or the fault of the copyists and typographers; but study, and the possession of some small stock of the knowledge by which he worked, will enable us often to detect and explain his meaning. He never wrote at random, or hit upon points of character and conduct by chance; and the smallest fragment of his mind not unfrequently gives a clue to a most perfect, regular, and consistent whole.

There is a notebook entry in which Coleridge defines the imagination as "the laboratory, in which Thought elaborates Essence into Existence." His exegesis of *The Tempest* is the utterance of a great poet capable of doing what other great poets could never do: formulating his greatness as a poet in philosophical prose:

The Tempest is a specimen of the purely romantic drama, in which the interest is not historical, or dependent upon fidelity of portraiture, or the natural connection of events, – but is a birth of the imagination, and rests only on the coaptation and union of the elements granted to, or assumed by, the poet. It is a species of drama which owes no allegiance to time or space, and in which, therefore, errors of chronology and geography – no mortal sins in any species – are venial faults, and count for nothing. It addresses itself entirely to the imaginative faculty; and although the illusion may be assisted by the effect on the senses of the complicated scenery and decorations of modern times, yet this sort of assistance is dangerous. For the principal and only genuine excitement ought to come from within,– from the moved and sympathetic imagination; whereas, where so much is addressed to the mere external senses of seeing and hearing, the spiritual vision is apt to languish, and the attraction from without will withdraw the mind from the proper and only legitimate interest which is intended to spring from within.

7 Conclusion

The following is from a letter to William Sotheby (January 1803).
These are clearly the words of a man who, to borrow Walter Pater's
memorable phrase about the true aesthete's intensity of experience,
'burned always with a hard, gemlike flame':

> I never find myself at one within the embracement of rock &
> hills, a traveller up an alpine road, but my spirit courses, drives,
> and eddies, like a Leaf in Autumn: a wild activity, of thoughts,
> imaginations, feelings, and impulses of motion, rises up from
> within me – a sort of *bottom-wind*, that blows to no point of
> the compass, & comes from I know not whence, but agitates
> the whole of me; my whole Being is filled with waves, as it
> were, that roll & stumble, one this way, & one that way, like
> things that have no common master. I think that my soul must
> have pre-existed in the body of a Chamois-chaser ... The
> farther I ascend from animated Nature, from men, and cattle,
> & the common birds of the woods, & fields, the greater
> becomes in me the Intensity of feeling of Life ... In these
> moments it has been my creed, that Death exists only because
> Ideas exist: that Life is limitless Sensation; that Death is a
> child of the organic senses, chiefly of the Sight; that Feelings
> die by flowing into the mould of the Intellect ... I do not
> think it possible, that any bodily pains could eat out the love
> & joy, that is so substantially part of me, towards hills, &
> rocks, & steep waters! And I have had some Trial.

Coleridge was the walking, talking embodiment of the spirit of
Romanticism. He had the power to transfix listeners/readers with
the prolonged brightness of his propositions. The following, from
Section 2, Essay II of *The Friend*, is typically penetrating:

> Hast thou ever raised thy mind to the consideration of
> existence, in and by itself, as the mere act of existing? Hast
> thou ever said to thyself thoughtfully, It is! heedless in that
> moment, whether it were a man before thee, or a flower, or a
> grain of sand? without reference, in short, to this or that
> particular mode or form of existence? If thou hast attained to

this, thou wilt have felt the presence of a mystery, which must have fixed thy spirit in awe and wonder. The very words, There is nothing! or, There was a time when there was nothing! are self-contradictory. There is that within us which repels the proposition with as full and instantaneous a light, as if it bore evidence against the fact in the right of its own eternity.

Not to be, then, is impossible; to be, incomprehensible. If thou hast mastered this intuition of absolute existence, thou wilt have learnt likewise that it was this, and no other, which in the earlier ages seized the nobler minds, the elect among men, with a sort of sacred horror. This it was which first caused them to feel within themselves a something ineffably greater than their own individual nature.

I had intended to quote only a couple of sentences of the above, but I became entranced by Coleridge's metaphysics ...

In terms of how much he had read and understood, Coleridge had decades' worth more in him than anyone you care to think of. In terms of creative power, if he was not equal to Shakespeare, he was most certainly operating in that dizzying, stratospheric zone. For enthusiasts, enjoyment of his work often entails being "like a three years' child", compelled by the sheer authority of an 'adult thinker' who obviously sees further, and understands more. The arguments against Coleridge were first – and best – articulated by himself. His self-knowledge was, and is humbling. He wrote his own epitaph to which one might add without false acclaim: his like has not been seen, or heard, since.

EPITAPH

Stop, Christian passer-by! – Stop, child of God,
And read with gentle breast. Beneath this sod
A poet lies, or that which once seem'd he.
O, lift one thought in prayer for S.T.C.;
That he who many a year with toil of breath
Found death in life, may here find life in death!
Mercy for praise – to be forgiven for fame
He ask'd, and hoped, through Christ. Do thou the same!

Selected Bibliography

Editions

Coleridge: *Poems and Prose Selected by Kathleen Raine*
(Penguin, 1957) (Ideal for getting into STC Includes extracts
from *Biographia Literaria*, Shakespeare Lectures, letters, etc.)

Collected Letters of Samuel Taylor Coleridge, 6 vols., ed. E.L.
Griggs, (Oxford, 1956-71)

The Notebooks of Samuel Taylor Coleridge, 4 double vols., ed.
K. Coburn (vol. 4 edited by M. Christensen), (Bollingen Series,
Princeton University Press / Routledge, 1957-90)

Biographia Literaria, 2 vols., ed. J. Engell & W. Jackson Bate,
(Bollingen Series, Princeton University Press / Routledge,
1983)

Biographies

The Life of Samuel Taylor Coleridge: A Critical Biography,
R. Ashton (Blackwell, 1996)

Coleridge: Early Visions, R. Holmes (Hodder & Stoughton, 1989)

Coleridge: Darker Reflections, R. Holmes (HarperCollins, 1998)

Coleridge, The Damaged Archangel, N. Fruman (London, 1972)

Concerning Opium

Samuel Taylor Coleridge: A Bondage of Opium, Molly Lefebure,
(Gollancz, 1974)

Confessions of an English Opium-Eater, Thomas De Quincey,
1821 (Oxford, 1989)

STC and Science

What Coleridge Thought, O. Barfield (Oxford, 1972) 'A Bridge
Between Science and Poetry', K. Coburn in *Coleridge's Variety:
Bicentenary Studies*, ed. J. Beer (Macmillan, 1974)

More about STC

A History of Modern Criticism: 1750-1950, René Wellek (New Haven, 1955)

The Road to Xanadu, J. Livingston Lowes, 1927 (Picador, 1978)

'Literary Gentlemen and Lovely Ladies: The Debate on the Character of "Christabel"', K. Swann in *Romanticism*, ed. C. Chase (Longman, 1993)

Poets Through Their Letters, Martin Seymour-Smith (Constable, 1969)

(The last essay is on Coleridge.)

More General

Romantics, Rebels & Reactionaries, M. Butler (Oxford, 1981)

Romantic Affinities, R. Christiansen, (Vintage, 1994)

Greenwich Exchange Books

STUDENT GUIDES

Greenwich Exchange Student Guides are critical studies of major or contemporary serious writers in English and selected European languages. The series is for the student, the teacher and 'common readers' and is an ideal resource for libraries. The *Times Educational Supplement* (*TES*) praised these books saying, "The style of these guides has a pressure of meaning behind it. Students should learn from that... If art is about selection, perception and taste, then this is it."

(ISBN prefix 1-871551- applies)
The series includes:
W. H. Auden by Stephen Wade (-36-6)
Balzac by Wendy Mercer (48-X)
William Blake by Peter Davies (-27-7)
The Brontës by Peter Davies (-24-2)
Joseph Conrad by Martin Seymour-Smith (-18-8)
William Cowper by Michael Thorn (-25-0)
Charles Dickens by Robert Giddings (-26-9)
John Donne by Sean Haldane (-23-4)
Ford Madox Ford by Anthony Fowles (63-3)
Thomas Hardy by Sean Haldane (-33-1)
Seamus Heaney by Warren Hope (-37-4)
Philip Larkin by Warren Hope (-35-8)
Laughter in the Dark – The Plays of Joe Orton by Arthur Burke (56-0)
Shakespeare's Non-Dramatic Poetry by Martin Seymour-Smith (22-6)
Shakespeare's Sonnets by Martin Seymour Smith (38-2)
Tobias Smollett by Robert Giddings (-21-8)
Alfred Lord Tennyson by Michael Thorn (-20-X)
Wordsworth by Andrew Keanie (57-9)

OTHER GREENWICH EXCHANGE BOOKS
Paperback unless otherwise stated.

English Language Skills *by Vera Hughes*
If you want to be sure, as a student, or in your business or personal life, that your written English is correct and up-to-date, this book is for you. Vera Hughes's aim is to help you remember the basic rules of spelling, grammar

and punctuation. 'Noun', 'verb', 'subject', 'object' and 'adjective' are the only technical terms used. The book teaches the clear, accurate English required by the business and office world, coaching in acceptable current usage, and making the rules easier to remember.

With a degree in modern languages and trained as a legal secretary, Vera Hughes went from the City into training with the retail industry before joining MSC as a Senior Training Advisor. As an experienced freelance trainer, she has worked at all levels throughout the UK and overseas, training business people in communication skills, but specialising in written business English. As former Regional Manager for RSA Examinations Board, she is also aware of the needs of students in schools and colleges. Her sound knowledge of English and her wide business experience are an ideal combination for a book about basic English language skills.

ISBN 1-871551-60-9; A5 size; 142pp

LITERATURE & BIOGRAPHY

The Author, the Book & the Reader *by Robert Giddings*

This collection of essays analyses the effects of changing technology and the attendant commercial pressures on literary styles and subject matter. Authors covered include Dickens, Smollett, Mark Twain, Dr Johnson, John Le Carré.

ISBN 1-871551-01-3; A5 size; 220pp; illus.

The Good That We Do *by John Lucas*

John Lucas' new book blends fiction, biography and social history in order to tell the story of the grandfather he never knew. Horace Kelly was born in Torquay in 1880 and died 60 years later, soon after the outbreak of the World War II. Headteacher of a succession of elementary schools in impoverished areas of London during the first part of the 20th Century, 'Hod' Kelly was also a keen cricketer, a devotee of the music hall, and included among his friends the great Trade Union leader, Ernest Bevin. In telling the story of his life, Lucas has provided a fascinating range of insights into the lives of ordinary Londoners: their entertainments, domestic arrangements, experiences of the privations of war, including the aerial bombardments of 1917 and 1918, and their growing realisation during the 20s and 30s that they were doomed to suffer it all again. Threaded through is an account of such people's hunger for education, and of the different ways government, church and educational officialdom ministered to that hunger. *The Good That We Do* is both a study of one man and of a period when England changed, drastically and for ever.

ISBN 1-871551-54-4; A5 size; 213pp

In Pursuit of Lewis Carroll *by Raphael Shaberman*
Sherlock Holmes and the author uncover new evidence in their invest-igations into the mysterious life and writing of Lewis Carroll. They examine published works by Carroll that have been overlooked by previous commentators. A newly discovered poem, almost certainly by Carroll, is published here. Amongst many aspects of Carroll's highly complex personality, this book explores his relationship with his parents, numerous child friends, and the formidable Mrs Liddell, mother of the immortal Alice. ISBN 1-871551-13-7; 70% A4 size; 118pp; illus.

Laughter in the Dark – The Plays of Joe Orton *by Arthur Burke*
Arthur Burke examines the two facets of Joe Orton. Orton the playwright had a rare ability to delight and shock audiences with such outrageous farces as *Loot* and *What the Butler Saw*. Orton the man was a promiscuous homosexual caught up in a destructive relationship with a jealous and violent older man. In this study – often as irreverent as the plays themselves – Burke dissects Orton's comedy and traces the connection between the lifestyle and the work. Previously a television critic and comedian, Arthur Burke is a writer and journalist. He has published articles not only on Orton but also on Harold Pinter, John Osborne and many other leading modern dramatists.
ISBN 1-981551-56-0; A5 size; 97pp

Liar! Liar!: Jack Kerouac – Novelist *by R.J. Ellis*
The fullest study of Jack Kerouac's fiction to date. It is the first book to devote an individual chapter to each and every one of his novels. *On the Road, Visions of Cody* and *The Subterraneans*, Kerouac's central masterpieces, are re-read in depth, in a new and exciting way. The books Kerouac himself saw as major elements of his spontaneous 'bop' odyssey, *Visions of Gerard* and *Doctor Sax*, are also strikingly reinterpreted, as are other, daringly innovative writings, like 'The Railroad Earth' and his "try at a spontaneous *Finnegans Wake*" – *Old Angel Midnight*. Undeservedly neglected writings, such as *Tristessa* and *Big Sur*, are also analysed, alongside better known novels like *Dharma Bums* and *Desolation Angels*. *Liar! Liar!* takes its title from the words of *Tristessa's* narrator, Jack, referring to himself. He also warns us "I guess, I'm a liar, watch out!" R.J. Ellis' study provocatively proposes that we need to take this warning seriously and, rather than reading Kerouac's novels simply as fictional versions of his life, focus just as much on the way the novels stand as variations on a series of ambiguously-represented themes: explorations of class, sexual identity, the French-Canadian Catholic confessional, and addiction in its hydra-headed modern forms. Ellis shows how Kerouac's

deep anxieties in each of these arenas makes him an incisive commentator on his uncertain times and a bitingly honest self-critic, constantly attacking his narrators' 'vanities'.

R.J. Ellis is Professor of English and American Studies at the Nottingham Trent University. His commentaries on Beat writing have been frequently published, and his most recent book, a full modern edition of Harriet Wilson's *Our Nig*, the first ever novel by an African-American woman, has been widely acclaimed.

ISBN 1-871551-53-6; A5 size; 295pp

Musical Offering *by Yolanthe Leigh*

In a series of vivid sketches, anecdotes and reflections, Yolanthe Leigh tells the story of her growing up in the Poland of the 30s and World War II. These are poignant episodes of a child's first encounters with both the enchantments and the cruelties of the world; and from a later time, stark memories of the brutality of the Nazi invasion, and the hardships of student life in Warsaw under the Occupation. But most of all, this is a record of inward development; passages of remarkable intensity and simplicity describe the girl's response to religion, to music, and to her discovery of philosophy.

The outcome is something unique, a book that eludes classification. In its own distinctive fashion, it creates a memorable picture of a highly perceptive and sensitive individual, set against a background of national tragedy.

ISBN 1-871551-46-3; A5 size; 57pp

Norman Cameron *by Warren Hope*

Cameron's poetry was admired by Auden, celebrated by Dylan Thomas and valued by Robert Graves. He was described by Martin Seymour-Smith as: "one of ... the most rewarding and pure poets of his generation ..." and is at last given a full length biography. This eminently sociable man, who had periods of darkness and despair, wrote little poetry by comparison with others of his time, but always of a high and consistent quality – imaginative and profound.

ISBN 1-871551-05-6; A5 size; 221pp; illus.

Shakespeare's Non-Dramatic Poetry *by Martin Seymour-Smith*

In this study, completed shortly before his death in 1998, Martin Seymour-Smith sheds fresh light on two very different groups of Shakespeare's non-dramatic poems: the early and conventional *Venus and Adonis* and *The Rape of Lucrece*, and the highly personal *Sonnets*. He explains the genesis of the first two in the genre of Ovidian narrative poetry in which a young

Elizabethan man of letters was expected to excel, and which was highly popular. In the *Sonnets* (his 1963 old-spelling edition of which is being reissued by Greenwich Exchange) he traces the mental journey of a man going through an acute psychological crisis as he faces up to the truth about his own unconventional sexuality.

It is a study which confronts those 'disagreeables' in the *Sonnets* which most critics have ignored.
ISBN 1-871551-22-6; A5 size; 84pp

Shakespeare's Sonnets *edited by Martin Seymour-Smith*
Martin Seymour-Smith's outstanding achievement lies in the field of literary biography and criticism. In 1963 he produced his comprehensive edition, in the old spelling, of *Shakespeare's Sonnets* (here revised and corrected by himself and Peter Davies in 1998). With its landmark introduction, it was praised by William Empson and John Dover Wilson. Stephen Spender said of him: "I greatly admire Martin Seymour-Smith for the independence of his views and the great interest of his mind" and both Robert Graves and Anthony Burgess described him as the leading critic of his time. His exegesis of the Sonnets remains unsurpassed.
ISBN 1-871551-38-2; A5 size; 200pp

POETRY
Adam's Thoughts in Winter *by Warren Hope*
Warren Hope's poems have appeared from time to time in a number of literary periodicals, pamphlets, and anthologies on both sides of the Atlantic. They appeal to lovers of poetry everywhere. His poems are brief, clear, frequently lyrical, characterised by wit, but often distinguished by tenderness. The poems gathered in this first book-length collection counter the brutalising ethos of contemporary life, speaking of and for the virtues of modesty, honesty, and gentleness in an individual, memorable way. Hope was born in Philadelphia where he raised his family and continues to live near there. He is the author of critical studies of Shakespeare and Larkin and is the biographer of Norman Cameron, the British poet and translator.
ISBN 1-871551-40-4; A5 size; 47pp

Baudelaire: Les Fleurs du Mal in English Verse *translated by F.W. Leakey*
Selected poems from *Les Fleurs du Mal* are translated with parallel French texts and designed to be read with pleasure by readers who have no French, as well as those practised in the French language.

F.W. Leakey is Emeritus Professor of French in the University of London. As a scholar, critic and teacher he has specialised in the work of Baudelaire for 50 years. He has published a number of books on Baudelaire.
ISBN 1-871551-10-2; A5 size; 153pp

Lines from the Stone Age *by Sean Haldane*

Reviewing Sean Haldane's 1992 volume *Desire in Belfast* Robert Nye wrote in *The Times* that "Haldane can be sure of his place among the English poets." The fact that his early volumes appeared in Canada and that he has earned his living by means other than literature have meant that this place is not yet a conspicuous one, although his poems have always had their circle of readers. The 60 previously unpublished poems of *Lines from the Stone Age* – "lines of longing, terror, pride, lust and pain" – may widen this circle.

ISBN 1-871551-39-0; A5 size; 53pp

Wilderness *by Martin Seymour-Smith*

This is Seymour-Smith's first publication of his poetry for more than 20 years. This collection of 36 poems is a fearless account of an inner life of love, frustration, guilt, laughter and the celebration of others. Best known to the general public as the author of the controversial and best selling *Hardy* (1994).

ISBN 1-871551-08-0; A5 size; 52pp

PHILOSOPHY

Deals and Ideals *by James Daly*

Alasdair MacIntyre writes of this book: "In his excellent earlier book *Marx: Justice and Dialectic* James Daly identified Marx's place in and extraordinary contribution to the moral debates of the modern era. Now he has put us even further in his debt not only by relating Marx to his Aristotelian predecessors and to the natural law tradition, but also by using this understanding of Marx to throw fresh light on the moral antagonism between Marx and individualist conceptions of human nature. This is a splendid sequel to his earlier work."

ISBN 1-87155-31-5; A5 size; 156pp

Marx: Justice and Dialectic *by James Daly*

Department of Scholastic Philosophy, Queen's University, Belfast.

James Daly shows the humane basis of Marx's thinking, rather than the imposed 'economic materialistic' views of many modern commentators. In particular he refutes the notion that for Marx, justice relates simply to the state of development of society at a particular time. Marx's views about justice and human relationships belong to the continuing traditions of moral thought in Europe.

ISBN 1-871551-28-5; A5 size; 144pp

The Philosophy of Whitehead *by T.E. Burke*
Department of Philosophy, University of Reading.
Dr Burke explores the main achievements of this philosopher, better known in the US than Britain. Whitehead, often remembered as Russell's tutor and collaborator on *Principia Mathematica,* was one of the few who had a grasp of relativity and its possible implications. His philosophical writings reflect his profound knowledge of mathematics and science. He was responsible for initiating process theology.
ISBN 1-871551-29-3; A5 size; 101pp

Questions of Platonism *by Ian Leask*
In a daring challenge to contemporary orthodoxy, Ian Leask subverts both Hegel and Heidegger by arguing for a radical re-evaluation of Platonism. Thus, while he traces a profoundly Platonic continuity between ancient Athens and 19th century Germany, the nature of this Platonism, he suggests, is neither 'totalizing' nor Hegelian but, instead, open-ended, 'incomplete' and oriented towards a divine goal beyond *logos* or any metaphysical structure. Such a re-evaluation exposes the deep anti-Platonism of Hegel's absolutizing of volitional subjectivity; it also confirms Schelling as true modern heir to the 'constitutive incompletion' of Plato and Plotinus. By providing a more nuanced approach – refusing to accept either Hegel's self-serving account of 'Platonism' or the (equally totalizing) post-Heideggerian inversion of this narrative – Leask demonstrates the continued relevance of a genuine, 'finite' Platonic quest. Ian Leask teaches in the Department of Scholastic Philosophy at the Queen's University of Belfast.
ISBN 1-871551-32-3; A5 size; 154pp

FICTION
The Case of the Scarlet Woman – Sherlock Holmes and the Occult
by Watkin Jones
A haunted house, a mysterious kidnapping and a poet's demonic visions are just the beginnings of three connected cases that lead Sherlock Holmes into confrontation with the infamous black magician Aleister Crowley and, more sinisterly, his scorned Scarlet Woman.

The fact that Dr Watson did not publish details of these investigations is perhaps testament to the unspoken fear he and Holmes harboured for the supernatural. *The Case of the Scarlet Woman* convinced them both that some things cannot be explained by cold logic.
ISBN 1-871551-14-5; A5 size; 124pp

MISCELLANEOUS

Music Hall Warriors: A history of the Variety Artistes Federation
by Peter Honri

This is an unique and fascinating history of how vaudeville artistes formed the first effective actors' trade union in 1906 and then battled with the powerful owners of music halls to obtain fairer contracts. The story continues with the VAF dealing with performing rights, radio, and the advent of television. Peter Honri is the fourth generation of a vaudeville family. The book has a foreword by the Rt Hon. John Major MP when he was Prime Minister – his father was a founder member of the VAF.

ISBN 1-871551-06-4; A4 size; 140pp; illus.